The School Library Media Specialist's Tool Kit

Richard C. Pearson

With Kaye Y. Turner

 **Highsmith Press Handbook Series**

Fort Atkinson, Wisconsin

Published by Highsmith Press LLC
W5527 Highway 106
P.O. Box 800
Fort Atkinson, Wisconsin 53538-0800
1-800-558-2110

© Richard C. Pearson, 1999
Cover by Alison Relyea

The paper used in this publication meets the minimum requirements of
American National Standard for Information Science —
Permanence of Paper for Printed Library Material. ANSI/NISO Z39.48-1984.

Library of Congress Cataloging-in-Publication Data
Pearson, Richard C., 1938–
    The school library media specialist's tool kit / Richard C.
Pearson, with Kaye Turner.
      p.   cm. -- (Highsmith Press handbook series)
    Includes bibliographical references and index.
    ISBN 1-57950-012-9 (paper : alk. paper)
    1. School libraries--United States. 2. Instructional materials
centers--United States. I. Turner, Kaye Y. II. Title.
III. Series.
Z675.S3P33 1999
025.5' 678222' 0973--dc21   98-39810
                              CIP

Contents

Preface

Africa – wood

This handbook is the result of some twenty-five years of hands-on, in-the-trenches school librarianship. It is intended as a tool kit for elementary and secondary school librarians. A good tool kit contains many tools, quickly accessible, which enables one to complete a job and possibly, within the process, create something wonderful. While specifically written for school librarians, many chapters deal with topics common to all libraries. The reader is invited to explore the contents and use those tools which will best improve library services for their many and varied patrons.

We would like to acknowledge contributions of many fine school librarians leading toward the completion of this handbook. Several have contributed chapters in their areas of expertise and others have helped edit and give direction. Special appreciation to Don Sager, Highsmith Press, for his many valuable suggestions.

The first hurdle to overcome in the handbook was how to refer to the many different titles used by school librarians and the school library facility. Media Generalists? Media Specialist? Media/Librarian? Media Center? Instructional Media Center? Learning Center? He? She? The list goes on and on. For reasons of clarity and ease of reading we chose the terms librarian and library. Since the vast majority of school librarians are women, the pronoun she is used when necessary. This is not meant to exclude the many excellent men in the field.

Another question was how to best illustrate the book. Masks from around the world were chosen to illustrate each chapter because they symbolically represent the emotions, concerns, humor, and other facets of school librarianship. Their cultural and visual message is a powerful one, matching the impact that a fine school library will have upon the local community, the school, and ultimately upon student lives.

Throughout their professional careers the authors have never found a practical, comprehensive guide to school librarianship. It is our intention to provide this book as a tool kit for experienced school librarians and for those just entering this exciting, ever-changing career.

National Standards for Information Literacy

Throughout America, schools are now designing curriculums and teaching courses that will achieve a variety of standards. These are goals to be reached and skills students are to attain as they complete classes and continue through the educational process. Many of these standards have been developed by librarians, educators, and subject-area specialists. The use of standards has been most successful when those involved in their development have worked closely with the parents and communities in which students reside. Standards which reflect local values and skills are having a tremendous impact upon student achievement. Teaching to standards is the wave of the future, and it is already being done in many fields of study.

One particularly relevant new set of national standards was announced by the American Association of School Librarians (AASL) during the 117th Annual ALA Conference in June, 1998. Developed in concert with the Association for Educational Communications and Technology (AECT), these standards are intended to improve information literacy among students from kindergarten through twelfth-grade. The set of nine standards will guide school librarians and educators in cultivating and refining students' information literacy skills in print, non-print and electronic formats, all of which will be essential skills in the 21st century and beyond. "Student achievement is the bottom line," says Kenneth Haycock, president of AASL. "Knowing how to obtain and use and use information properly is increasingly essential both for the students' success in school and for their personal and professional development as socially responsible adults."[1]

The standards cover three major areas: information literacy, independent learning, and social responsibility. Each standard includes "success indicators" and "levels of proficiency" to help educators to determine a student's level of achievement.

It behooves every school librarian to use these standards as parameters as they guide the library towards supporting and enhancing the school's curricula and educational mission. Indeed, all functions of the library should reflect and teach towards these national standards for information literacy.

Notes
1. ALA Public Information Office. News Release. Chicago: ALA, July 7, 1998.
2. Ibid.

Information Literacy

Standard 1: The student who is information literate accesses information efficiently and effectively.

Standard 2: The student who is information literate evaluates information critically and completely.

Standard 3: The student who is information literate uses information accurately and creatively.

Independent Learning

Standard 4: The student who is an independent learner is information literate and pursues information related to personal interests.

Standard 5: The student who is an independent learner is information literate and appreciates literature and other creative expressions of information.

Standard 6: The student who is an independent learner is information literate and strives for excellence information seeking and knowledge generation.

Social Responsibility

Standard 7: The student who contributes positively to the learning community and to society is information literate and recognizes the importance of information to a democratic society.

Standard 8: The student who contributes positively to the learning community and to society is information literate and practices ethical behavior in regard to information and information technology.

Standard 9: The student who contributes positively to the learning community and to society is information literate and participates effectively in groups to pursue and generate information.[2]

Chapter One

Introducing Children to Reading & Libraries

Ginina Dugdale

India – paper maché

"Are there any good books in this library?"
"There aren't any good books in this library."
"I've read all the books in this library."

What librarian hasn't heard one of these statements? Often they come from a young, reluctant or frustrated reader. Children are not born with the skill of browsing, and they are often overwhelmed with the prospect of selecting the right book from shelves and shelves of books, especially if they are not good readers. It is the librarian's job to have books in the collection for all levels of readers and then develop strategies to connect the students with the book that is "just right," not one time, but week after week, year after year, until they are confident and competently selecting the right books.

Emergent Readers

Most elementary school libraries have extensive picture book/easy sections. But books in this area encompass a wide range of reading levels. Unless books are pulled from the shelves it will be next to impossible for most first graders, or other emergent readers, to find books they can read. There are sets of emergent reading books on the market now that are very good. These books can be marked (with a large blue sticker, for example) and set aside on a special shelf or in a plastic tub, box, or bin, making them easily accessible for emergent readers to check out.

Allowing students in the first through sixth grades to check out at least two books gives the librarian the leverage to expect that one of the books is a "just right" book. It is important to stress this point with students.

Second Graders

Second grade is a great time to begin an aggressive campaign of choosing books that are readable. Tell students to think about this; if they start checking out chapter books that are too hard, the book will just sit in their desk, unread. Soon, they will be in the habit of checking out books and not reading them. What a tragedy! What a waste! Second graders have a big assignment.

Many of them are making the leap from picture books to chapter books, but they cannot go from a 32-page book to a 126-page book overnight. Tell them this. For most students this needs to be done in small steps and the librarian plays a crucial role in the process. Again, it is vital to pull books from the collection and set them off on their own shelves or cart. A gold star on the spine can designate this category of easy chapter books. These books have very likely been sitting on the shelves for years, mostly unread. But put a gold star on the spine, read aloud from a few of them to the classes, get excited, *and these books will be hot items.* The young readers will develop a sense of self-confidence, knowing they can now read a book with approximately 64 pages. They will love it.

Pull out those old Dolch books and read a story or two aloud to classes. There will be some students who will love them.

What are these books?

They are all about the same size and format. Authors include Benchley, Bonsall, Browne, Hoff, Lobel, Parish, Rylant, and Sharmat to name just a few. Some come from the Now I Can Read series. A systematic trip through the shelves should net a sizeable collection to get started with.

Of course, there will be some second graders already reading chapter books. From second through sixth grades, the librarian's chief joy and satisfaction comes from staying one jump ahead of the voracious reader. What a challenge! But these students are easy, because if the librarian doesn't have time for them, they are perfectly capable of finding their own books and will often recommend new ones for purchase.

What about that feisty, renegade second grader who can just barely read *Nate the Great*, but insists on checking out a two-hundred-page novel? Does the librarian expect, suggest, recommend, or insist that an easier book accompany that student out of the library? Although suggestions and recommendations work for some students, there are others who need a more assertive approach. Librarians cannot stand by in this day and age and expect all students to know what to check out. The influence of television and broken homes alone brings us a population of children who may not have had much guidance in leisure reading, much less book selection. However, it is not simply a matter of rejecting a student's choice. This decision must be accompanied by love and tact. The student needs to be left with a sense of teamwork taking place, rather than an authoritarian decision being handed down.

Give students the five finger rule. They read a page from their book, putting up a finger every time they come across a word they cannot pronounce or understand. If five fingers are up at the end of the page the book is too hard. If four fingers are up but they don't understand what was read, the book is too hard. Listening to individual students read, gives the librarian the opportunity to jot down notes, make title recommendations, and steer the students toward harder or easier books. How and when is time found to listen to students read? About a month into the school year inform classes that rather than the librarian reading to the students, the students are going to read to the librarian. Make it clear that it is going to take time to get to each student so the amount of reading done by them may be only a paragraph or a page. They need to understand that listening to them read is enjoyable but their reading will be limited to permit all students to have this opportunity. Once all students have been listened to, a copy of the list of names with brief notes can be kept at the checkout counter. The person who checks out books can use this as a reference. Students need to know that their librarians are going to be adamant about them checking out books they can read! Once the habit is begun, it is very satisfying to watch these young readers become more thoughtful and careful about their book selection. They will become adamant themselves about checking out books they can read. Another bonus of the one-on-one reading time is that it gives the librarian the opportunity to bond with each student. The child who may not have the courage to seek their librarian's advise is going to be a lot more comfortable asking for help after a few minutes of sitting side by side and reading together.

Third Graders

The same basic strategy should be used with third graders. Listen to them read, stressing the five finger rule and the importance of selecting a book they can read. For second and third grades the "gold star" books are very important, but it is necessary to provide them with the next step. Once the "gold star" books are too easy, then it is time to move on to short chapter books. Again, it works well to pull books from the collection and label the spine. Because some librarians may choose to keep these books on the shelves with the other fiction books a red star works well because it is easily seen. These should be books that are 60 to 80 pages long with large print, big margins, and some pictures. The Stepping Stone series is an example of excellent,

Students enjoy reading in a space that lends itself to the imagination. A boat, a train or old bathtub offer a creative, comfortable space for leisure reading.

Encourage students to come back and let you know when the books they are reading have become too easy. Listen to them read again, make suggestions and adjust notes. Ideally the librarian will listen to all second and third graders read twice each year.

easy chapter books. When students are ready to move from these books, it is wise to have a bank of authors ready for recommendation. Cleary, Erickson, Christopher, and Warner are but a few possibilities.

When students realize that their reading selection is a team effort, they will come to the librarian often for advice. They need to be encouraged to come back for more ideas when they are ready to move on to something more challenging.

Fourth Through Sixth Graders

If the reading selection program has been successful with the second and third graders, by fourth grade most students should be well on their way to being independent readers with good book selection habits. Until a few years ago, there was never a question as to whether a student "had" to check out a book. But that question seems to be occurring more frequently. Most classroom teachers will support a librarian's decision to expect all older students to check out a minimum of one chapter book per week. Some librarians may choose to peruse the class line as students are leaving the library to see what students have selected. Others may leave that up to the classroom teacher with an invitation to send students back who have not checked out a chapter book. Be careful and thoughtful when presenting these guidelines to students. The librarian is in a powerful position to influence students' reading in either a positive or negative way. Again, it is important that this does not come across as an authoritarian, negative decision, but rather a decision made with firmness, love and tact in the interest of helping each student on a path to enjoyable, lifelong, leisure reading.

Encourage students in second grade on up not to abandon picture books. They can be enjoyed for a lifetime.

Library Skills

How and when are library skills taught? The most obvious answer is to teach them when students need them. Ideally students would be taught how to use the card catalog and CD-ROM encyclopedia when they are researching a report, and the arrangement of the fiction collection when they are intent on finding a specific book. Unfortunately, few librarians have the luxury of working with small groups of students, so it is difficult to accomplish this. Large student populations, time constraints, and limited staff prevent many librarians from instituting the flexible scheduling which would allow library skills to be taught at the golden moment when they are needed.

So, how and when are library skills to be taught? When possible, go for the gold at the teachable moment, but if that is not possible, the most important thing is to have a skills curriculum that is dynamic, innovative, and hands on. Librarians must be outstanding teachers if students are going to develop into independent lifelong learners. Students need to know their librarian likes them, indeed loves them, and cares deeply about their intellectual growth. The first step in teaching these skills is to give students a clear statement of expectations: "I want you to understand how to use the computerized catalog (or how the fiction and non-fiction areas are arranged). This will allow you to walk into any library and feel comfortable finding your way around."

*The label of **E**asy for a whole section of the library effectively deters older students from using it because of the stigma associated with its name. Why not call this section **E**verybody?*

There are many library skills curricula on the market, so the full range of library skills will not be addressed here. Perhaps the most important thing to remember when teaching skills is to make them directly involve the library's collection. Students have enough dittos and work sheets in their lives without adding more in the library.

Call Numbers and Spine Labels—*What's the Connection?*

One of the hardest concepts to get across to elementary-age students is the connection between the call number and the spine label. The notion that the first one helps find the second is missed by many students. This idea can be introduced by referring to the cart of books waiting to be re-shelved. Pose this question: How do librarians know where to put books back on the shelf? Do they look at the covers and guess? Explain that the spine labels make it simple. Use a variety of books to demonstrate this and let them know you think this is an extraordinarily clever system. Give students cards with sample call numbers from one area of the library and have them locate a matching spine label on the shelves. Follow up with a different area the next week. The third week shuffle the deck in front of the class, pass out the cards and see what happens. Can they locate the spine label using the call number? If it clicks, then the call numbers on the catalog screen are going to make sense.

It will be the librarian's eternal quest to pursue easier and smoother ways to teach library skills focused on the relevancy of each situation. Our responsibility is to keep fine tuning the procedure so it is enjoyable and easily understood by all.

Start first graders with finding a letter on the shelves in the Easy (Everybody) section. Review this with second graders then assign them to find their spot on the shelf if they were the author. Where would their last name be located? Are there any authors with the same last name?

Reference Books or The Great Pickle Race

"Do we get to do the Great Pickle Race this year?" is a commonly asked question when this method is used to teach encyclopedia, atlas, almanac, thesaurus, and dictionary skills. The goal of the Race is to teach and reinforce the use of reference books though repetition in a relevant and exciting way.

Preparation for the Race

1. Using the word processor, numbered questions are printed on bright green paper which is then laminated and cut into pickle shapes. *(See the sample pickles on the next page.)* For example, atlas questions could be numbered 1–50, with 1–25 being easier and 26–50 more difficult.

2. Have one set of questions for third and fourth graders and a harder set for fifth and sixth graders.

3. Have a special set of questions on a different shade of green that are "hot pickle" questions for those who really want to be challenged.

4. Gather empty pickle jars so questions for each set of skills, atlas, almanac, etc., can be kept in their own labeled jar. This makes it easy to grab a jar depending on what grade level and skill is needed. If the jars still smell like pickles, so much the better.

5. Have class lists, with a grid, printed on a computer from the library or office.

6. Suspend a "Great Pickle Race Headquarters" sign above a designated table which will allow the librarian to be seated so she can see the rest of the library and monitor students not actively involved in the Race.

7. For consistency, it is helpful to have classroom sets of world almanacs and atlases.

8. For prizes, purchase or make a variety of bookmarks. Collect as many free or inexpensive items as possible, such as polished or cut rocks, small gourds and sea shells. Save posters and cards from *Sports Illustrated for Kids* or other high interest promotional materials.

9. Get large dill pickles for prizes. Explore the possibility of the PTA/PTO or Student Council providing the money for the purchase of pickles. Sometimes local supermarkets will donate jars of pickles.

Another organizational method is to have a folder with labeled pockets for each category of questions. Pull a set of questions and place them in the pickle jar as needed.

Logistics of Running the Race

There are many different ways to "run" the Great Pickle Race. One approach is to teach a skill for a specific reference book and then reinforce the lesson in small groups with the Race. Another approach is to teach all of the necessary skill lessons, and then let the race begin for all students for every reference book. Students come to the Great Pickle Race Headquarters where they remove a question from the jar, look it up and show the librarian the answer. The pickle number is then entered by the librarian, in the first box of the grid. Students are required to answer a minimum number of questions depending on the skills the librarian wants to teach and time constraints involved.

So far this does not sound too exciting, but now the fun begins, because students who wish to continue beyond the minimum number of questions are allowed to work on the Race whenever their class is in the library. It becomes something of a free-for-all but the excitement is truly something to behold. Why do they want to participate? When five questions have been answered students get to select a bookmark. When ten questions have been answered they earn a dill pickle to eat right in the library. Have small green pickle cutouts that can be given to students to turn in to the library assistant for a dill pickle. A fork to remove pickles from the jar and a piece of paper towel around the pickles is all that is needed for dispensing. Students will eat them on the spot. Be prepared for a few students to ask for the pickle juice! If fifteen questions are answered, the reward can be the polished rocks, sea shells, small dried gourds or posters. The rewards for fifteen, twenty or twenty-five questions do not get bigger and better but there is compensation for every five questions answered. A designated mark on the grid will keep track of which students have earned rewards. It is amazing what kids will do for a pickle or a polished rock!

Students participating in the Race also have an obligation to those who are reading. It is possible to keep the noise level at a whisper so others can have Time to Read In Peace. (TRIP time is an acronym that can be suggested to classroom teachers. It sounds more exciting and user friendly than sustained silent reading.)

Management of the Race, or How To Keep Chaos from Reigning!

Those students not participating in the Race should be getting books, or sitting and reading. Explain that if there are problems or a lack of cooperation, only one or two students will be able to participate at a time, so monitoring can be done by the librarian. This slows down the race and peer pressure usually brings everyone back in line. But if it doesn't, those students not following the rules can be asked to sit at a nearby table. Again, be sure expectations are clearly outlined, down to the smallest detail, so students know what is expected of them. With careful planning the Great Pickle Race can be enjoyed by all.

Sample Pickles

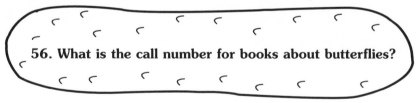

56. What is the call number for books about butterflies?

Online or card catalog

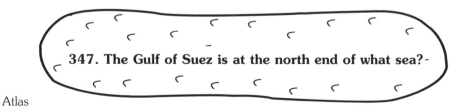

347. The Gulf of Suez is at the north end of what sea?-

Atlas

About the Author: Ginina Dugdale is school librarian at Tyhee and Greenacres Elementary Schools in Pocatello, Idaho. A native of New York, and a resident of southern Florida for several years, she earned her B.A. in elementary education from Idaho State University.

Chapter Two

Creating the Library's Ambiance

Brazil – clay

When people walk into a library, what is their first reaction? Indifference? Boredom? Surprise? Interest? What should their reaction be? Without realizing it, many libraries are visually boring, notwithstanding the architecture, which is often nondescript also. Because there are so many other responsibilities, decorating the library often falls on the shoulders of an assistant. Even with the best of intentions these decorations mostly center around one holiday each month or include mundane posters about books and reading. Throw in numerous signs to help locate areas of fiction and non-fiction and you have a good description of most librarians' decorating philosophy.

It is easy to fall into the trap of decorating with preprinted signs and posters purchased from catalogs or teacher stores. Handmade signs and hangings can be attractive and also have an initial visual impact on the patron, but how do they influence learning? What is the point of spending time and money every month of the year on things that are "cute" but worthless in the students' education?

Monthly Celebrations

October

For example, every year on the first of October most teachers and librarians bring out the pumpkins, the scarecrows, the cobwebs and the Happy Halloween signs. The rest of the month is then spent wondering why the students are so hyper about Halloween! There is a general move away from this holiday, but it serves as a starting point. Masks are a part of Halloween, but masks are also a part of most cultures. Decorating with masks in October allows the librarian to talk about celebrations, theater, dance, ceremony, and occupational masks, to name just a few possibilities. It also opens the door for discussions of materials: clay, fibers, wood, paper maché, and metal. And it becomes an invitation for students to bring in masks they may have at home. Along with those masks come the stories that go along with them. Students can be asked to make masks to decorate the library walls. A piece of masking tape with the student's name and room number on the back will assure the return of everything at the end of the month. Displaying masks from around the world makes it easy to slip in quick geography lessons. A globe should always be in the instructional area of the library. Not everyone will have a ready-made mask collection but a wise librarian will involve the faculty and friends. Starting with three or four masks, the seed will be planted and the students will take care of the rest. When their masks are displayed in the library, interest will be piqued, and the big question will then be, "What are we going to do next month?"

November

November is a great month to decorate with food. In Southeast Idaho, it is easy to drive to Willard, Utah, and have access to vegetable stands with banana squash three to four feet long; bumpy gnarled hubbard squash weighing 45 to 50 pounds; colorful Turks cap squash and numerous others, as well as gourds. Look for enormous size, interesting textures, and colors. The whole school will be taken by surprise when they walk in November 1, and find these treasures laying around on library

The Cram Map Company has a beautiful globe featuring colors very different from the standard globe seen in most schools. The colors alone draw students' attention to it.

Sources for materials include yard sales and second hand stores. Folks who are traveling to other countries could be a resource.

tables and counter tops. Hang Indian corn on the walls and discussion will abound. Discuss the difference between squash and gourds. What can be made out of gourds? Once again, objects and stories will flow into the library and the gardeners in the student body and faculty will surface. The Wednesday before Thanksgiving cut up all the squash and send it home with anyone who wants it.

December

Hang colorful material from different countries on the library's walls for December. One country at a time lends variety over the years and allows for different cultural explorations. Mexico works well because of the brightly woven textiles, including clothing, rugs and hammocks. Hanging piñatas and pictures of Mexico complete the scene. And, yes, once again objects and stories will flow into the library.

There are many other countries that work very well for decorating. Fiction and nonfiction books can be pulled that focus on the selected country to further extend the cultural celebration. A locked glass display case is a good idea for small objects that may be too tempting, but experience has shown that students are very respectful of items brought in because of their own involvement.

January

January tends to be less hectic after the holidays and in the northern parts of the country, time stretches out long and cold. Why not give everyone something to look forward to when they come back after the holiday break? Kids love animals, so make January a unique celebration each year. Set the stage and let the students bring the rest. There is a good chance the library staff will go crazy this month hanging up stuffed animals, but it is well worth the time. Animals that librarians have used with great success are bears, cats (wild and domestic), the dog family, elephants, horses, tropical rainforest animals and animals of the oceans. Endangered species discussions are automatic concerning many of these animals.

Any of these animal celebrations can be done with clever "reading" sayings such as, "Reading is the Cat's Meow" or "Bear Down on Reading." Keep in mind that using the word "beary" for "very" is teaching nothing. Experience has shown that not much attention is paid to the sayings; it's the animal that counts. If hooks can be suspended from the ceiling with fish line it makes it easy to hang the stuffed animals that are brought in. Two words of caution: don't hang the animals by their necks! Their owners take great offense to this practice. A discretely placed safety pin is unobservable and works great. Second, if possible, label the student's initials and room number with a felt tip marker on the small fabric tag attached to the animal. Masking tape doesn't always stick to fuzz.

Fiction and nonfiction books can be pulled for this month's reading. Stories to be read aloud can revolve around the animal of choice and interesting photos can be hung. This is a good time to do a school-wide reading program using footprints, fish cut-outs, or a tail extending from a poster or picture of the animal. Each time a book is read by a student or an adult, the title and reader's name is written on the footprint, or fish, or whatever, and hung up in the hall. Color coding by grade level, with an additional color for all adult readers in the school, creates an interesting study and colorful display. It is best to keep it a celebration of reading rather than a competition. Working together as a school, all the hallways will be decorated by the end of the month. Because this involves a lot of time hanging up everyone's reading record, use student help. Some teachers may volunteer to hang their classes' records but don't ask them to add this to their list of things to do. Make sure student helpers understand exactly where and how the items are to be hung. This reading celebration seems to be special if it is not done every year.

The tropical rainforest and ocean themes are visually impressive if fish net can be hung over an expanse of the library, using the existing fish line and hooks. It makes

The American Gourd Society, PO Box 274, Mt. Gilead, Ohio 43338-0274 is an invaluable resource for materials, ideas and people who are experts with gourds.

If a Christmas tree is part of the library's traditional December decorations, continue to put it up, but consider decorating it with items from the featured country.

Another January celebration features a rain forest theme.

a great background for leaves or sea weed, and stuffed animals can be draped or hung. For the ocean unit, large sheets of transparent, blue, lightweight plastic can be laid on top of the net to give the illusion of being under water.

February

Because January's celebration is such a big production, it is logical to keep February low key but interesting. Hats are one possibility, and they can be used to highlight a hat day sponsored by the student council. Displaying hats can also help students understand cultures from around the world. Other categories can include old hats, new hats, sports and occupational hats to name but a few. There are great stories to be read about hats, and again students and staff will bring in their own tales.

March, April, and May

March, of course, brings kites to mind and what is better than the real thing? End of the season sales and yard/garage sales can net a nice collection for a small amount of money. Appeals to students will usually bring in some kites, although they need to commit to leaving them for a few weeks so the librarian doesn't have to climb a ladder everyday to give them back. It is perfectly fine for kites to stay up into the first weeks of April. When they come down, umbrellas can go up until the end of May. What a visual treat! And opened umbrellas indoors serve as an opportunity to talk about superstitions. With both kites and umbrellas there can be quick discussions of materials, i.e., paper kites and umbrellas versus ones made of more rugged fabrics for other uses. Geography lessons come naturally, and again students will bring their own items into the library.

Umbrellas provide a magical, visually stimulating end to the school year.

June, August, and September

The end of the school year in June and the beginning of the school year in August or September, need to be kept low key because there is so much to be done in the library. The following suggestions are easy to put up, eye-catching, and provoke comment and discussion: gigantic dried weeds or reeds nailed or pinned to the wall; neckties arranged on a wall in a big circle or half circles; and fans made from paper, palm leaves or other materials.

A Change of Pace

For a complete alternative, the following sequence was used one year to tie in with a textile art grant at Jefferson Elementary School in Pocatello, Idaho. A bulletin to parents and staff stated the following:

> Traditionally, library displays have encouraged students to bring in items that reflect the theme of the month. Because students participate in assembling the monthly displays, they learn, celebrate, and share stories. Bringing objects to the library encourages and stimulates dialogue at school and at home. To expand this learning technique the library will be used to showcase a variety of textiles from around the world to show their importance in our lives. The historical significance of textiles will be included. Every effort will be made to show artisans of both genders and from as many ethnic backgrounds as possible. The textile themes for the school year will include:
>
> **September** - Displaying textiles such as baskets, nets, ropes and bundles of natural fibers will demonstrate textile arts as survival art.
>
> **October** - Clothing made from woven cloth by individuals and handmade hats and bags will be displayed. This will tie in with our traditional display of masks, using a scarecrow format to display the garments with masks for heads.

Whatever course of decorating the librarian takes, the question needs to be asked: *Will it enhance the learning of the student?*

Quilts not only represent a rich heritage but offer insight into form, texture and color.

November - Textiles of Indonesia (This could be Africa or any specific country from which the school has access to textiles.)

December - Knitting and crocheting

January - Quilts

February - Textiles of India and other parts of Asia

March - Weaving

April - Embroidery, appliqué, needlepoint, and latchhook

May - Rags! Rags! Rags!" (Rugs, sock dolls and animals, etc.)

A spruce, fir and pine cone collection in jars, highlights the plant section and is useful in classrooms.

Signage

Major areas of the library need to be clearly marked. The Fiction and Easy (or Everybody) sections need to have easily read designations on the shelves; but non-fiction has more possibilities. Most libraries abound with cute or clever signs designating different subjects but once a sign has been in place for a few months it tends to become invisible. Why have visual clutter no one pays attention to? Whenever there is a choice, use something real. It will make the library look more interesting and draw the students' attention to the books. Plus, teachers will come in to borrow the peacock feathers above the bird books, the fossilized rocks above the rock and mineral books, the snake skin, the giant coconut, the beaver gnawed stick or vertebrae, the model Navajo Hogan, the solar system model, or the scales above the chemistry books. But will the teachers bring these items back? Part of the whole philosophy is to nurture a sense of trust. Experience has shown that teachers, like the students are respectful of library treasures. Make this area hands-on where possible. The balsa wood dinosaur model, model of an atom, or hornet's nest can hang if they are fragile, but all of these items make it very easy to direct students to books. They also have the Dewey classification numbers to guide them.

We want our students to be lifelong learners. We need to surround them with things that will catch their interest and provoke questions. We need to surround them with things they can touch, feel, and examine. We need to surround them with things that are visually stimulating; with things that are real.

A library with lots of large, live plants will complete the atmosphere of a space that is comfortable, inviting, warm, and attractive.

Chapter Three

Discipline in the Library

Indonesia – wood

Sh, Sh, Sh, Shhhhhhhhhhhhhhh!
What librarian hasn't uttered this sound a thousand times over?
"Sh, you're being too noisy."
"Sh, stop talking and read."
"Sh, now settle down."
"Sh, do you want me to send you back to your class?"
"Sh, stop fooling around and get a book checked out."
Sh, Sh, Sh.

Some librarians today do not mind if children speak in normal voices. And some librarians insist on tomb-like silence, while others want a library full of activity, with a light whispering buzz. When and where do children learn how to use a library? A few are lucky enough to have years of experience before they get to school, but many students have never entered a library. Therefore, it is the school librarian's responsibility to teach these children how to use the library and behave properly in one. It is not our place to be frustrated with the behavior of students coming to the library, but it is our job to analyze the situation, decide what it should be, and determine how to get there. There are many discipline plans available for consideration. The following has been found to be very effective in an elementary setting and could be adjusted for a secondary setting.

Rick Dahlgren states, in his *Preventive Discipline Program*,[1] that students should not be disciplined for anything they have not been taught. Therefore, it is extremely important that the first three to four weeks of each year be spent teaching the behavior desired in the library. Although this seems like a lot of time, the investment is well worth it, because the remainder of the year can then be spent teaching and enjoying students rather than over-emphasizing discipline.

The key is to thoroughly teach the librarian's expectations. Model what is acceptable and what is not. Have the students demonstrate what is acceptable (never what is not). Teach them what procedure will be followed if they are not behaving according to the rules. They need to understand there will not be warning after warning. They have all demonstrated proper behavior so the librarian's job is to warn the student. For example, "Joe, I need you to stop talking and listen." Then give the student a moment to make a decision about their behavior. If the behavior continues, then the student needs to "refocus." This means taking a behavior form and going to a designated classroom to fill it out. (Sample forms are located at the end of this chapter.) This program works best if it is schoolwide, but if that is not possible it can still be used effectively in the library. As with all discipline programs the most important aspects are to be consistent, fair, and put the responsibility for behavior in the hands of the student. Do not forget students need to know that the person disciplining them likes them! This needs to be demonstrated every day, in every way. Show the kids their librarian cares! The following are possible things to think about:

- How should students enter the library? Quietly? Silently? In line? The librarian needs to think about what she wants and then communicate this to each class-

If the librarian is still teaching to the class when a student returns from filling out the refocus form, the student should stand off to the side or at the door and listen until motioned in by the librarian. Teaching is too valuable to be interrupted.

room teacher before students ever enter the library at the beginning of the year. As soon as students enter, reinforce expectations, praise them if it was done correctly, and take them back to the classroom and start over if it was not done properly. Practice until it is done the way it should be done. If classes are entering as a group, it is imperative for the librarian to be at the entrance as the students arrive. Quietly greeting individual students and giving praise for good behavior gets each class period off to a good start.

- Opening procedure. Take the time to explain exactly what will take place at the beginning of each library session and what behaviors are expected. Address the fact that the students spend a small portion of time each week in the library and an even smaller amount of time listening to their librarian; so that is exactly what they must be doing—listening. Enforce this! During the first few weeks, stop speaking abruptly, if someone turns to their neighbor. When their attention comes back, remind them that in the future there will be a warning and refocus for that behavior. (Do not refocus until your entire discipline program has been explained, modeled, and demonstrated.)

- Next? How should students leave the instructional area? In a wild charge for books and the check-out desk? In an orderly fashion with no talking? Again, the librarian must decide exactly what behaviors are wanted, then communicate those expectations to the students. Although it seems like overkill, have students demonstrate walking across the library, individually or in small groups. Make sure every student knows exactly what is wanted and have them "prove" they know how to do it.

- If sticks (paint stir sticks) are used to designate the spot on the shelf where books were removed, demonstrate their use, step by step, and have students do the same.

- How should students line up at the check-out desk? Where and how should they sit and read? How should they return back to class? All behaviors should be addressed, demonstrated, and practiced with firmness, kindness, and a sense of humor where possible. Make it fun. For example, dismiss students from the instructional area by the colors on their clothing, or months of birthdays, or types of books in their hands.

- Overview. Because most librarians see a large number of classes every week, it is difficult to remember what is said to each class at the beginning of the year when teaching all of the expected behaviors. Posterboard cards with key phrases (in bold type), displayed on an easel, can serve as notes. The following list includes some possibilities:

Week One

Welcome! (Most school libraries don't open for business the first week of school so let them know you are thrilled to finally have them in the library.)

Seating (Where, how, voices. Stay in line? Friends next to friends?)

Whisper (Explain why a whisper is important in a library. They are not being told not to talk, but to do it in a whisper. Is whispering easy? No!)

Sticks (How and why they are used needs to be explained and demonstrated.)

What happens if you hit... (Because paint stir sticks are often used, what are the consequences?)

Number of books (Number of books students are allowed to check out. Can they come back before next week if they finish their books?)

Checking out books (Explain where to line up and how to hand books to the person checking out.)

Paint stir sticks bright colors and keep them in a basket, copper pot or other interesting container. Containers located in each section of the library will help insure their use. (Hint: when painting, paint one end on both sides then hang it up on a clothesline to dry before painting the other end or patterns.) This could also be a classroom or student council project using latex paint donated by a local business.

If there is a limit to the number of books to be checked out, invite parents to check out additional books for their children to be read together at home. Older students should be allowed additional books when doing reports, research or special projects.

No running (Explain why)

Returning books (When and where)

Seating (Expectations for reading, versus visiting and running around; how many people on a beanbag or couch.)

Departure (where to line up and voice volume.)

Week Two

Explain the weekly procedure; for example, read the overdue list, explain what renewing means and how to do it, and what to do with books while the librarian is talking. Posterboard cards could include:

Seating, sticks, voices and check out (Review each briefly, reminding students not to be lazy and return sticks to the container and to check out books before sitting and reading so there is not a pile up at the computer when it is time to head back to class.)

Fire drill (Explain the procedure)

Back to school night (Discuss the fact that the same behavior in the library is expected at night as during the day. Elicit their help if younger brothers or sisters are misbehaving.)

Bookmarks (Show where they are located and why it is important to use them rather than a pen, pencil, ruler or notebook. Explain how a book is put together and why the spine has to be treated with tender loving care.)

By reading from a list of students with books still out, the librarian can communicate with and be aware of those students who are not returning books on time. But perhaps more important, praise can be given to those who are renewing. If they are renewing, they are reading!

Week Three (Two sets of posterboard cards will be useful.)

First-Third Grades

Lost books (Encourage students to come and check with their librarian if they think their book is lost because someone else may have returned it. Let them know it is just great that so many students at their school are so good about returning books they find on the ground or any place where a book should not be. Explain that a lost book may be just waiting for them in the library.

Books on carts (Encourage students to check out books that have not been re-shelved yet! Some of the best books are sitting there because other students have just returned them.)

Paperbacks (How are they shelved and labeled? If they are color coded, or in tubs, explain how they are to be returned to their spot, as sticks are usually not used with paperbacks.)

Just right books (Introduce the idea of checking out books they can read.)

Save a seat? Nope! (Not with a body or a book. On your feet, lose your seat.)

Magic glue (It works well to tell younger students to find a place to read after their book is checked out and then glue themselves down until it is time to leave the library. That magic glue will hold them in their place until they are asked to line up and then it miraculously dissolves!)

Waiting for students to come to the library to claim lost and found books is a great way to see if that student is responsible. Tell students it is a test, plus why "torture" themselves with worry when their book may be waiting for them, due to the action of a good Samaritan.

The person checking out books can actually dispense magic glue from an empty (or pretend) squeeze bottle and a "slech" sound

Fourth-Sixth Grades

Come prepared (If their book is left in the classroom then they will have to do without it during their library time. They may bring it in later and get a new book on their own time. This policy will halt the steady stream of students back to the classroom during library time.)

Lost books, Books on carts, Save a seat? Nope! (Each of these cards would have the same explanation used with the first-third grades.)

Paperbacks (Explain how paperbacks are shelved and the system for returning them to their proper spot.)

Computer use (If a computerized card catalog is used, restrictions may need to be imposed to keep some students from spending their entire library time looking up titles rather than going to the shelves.)

Remember, it is important to be consistent and remind students that their time in the library is short and therefore precious. No time should be wasted with misbehavior. The librarian looks forward to seeing each and every child during that short span and nothing should interfere with it. Sometimes it works well to talk to individual students privately before they come to the library.

What are the rewards? Keep a chart with each teacher's name and enough squares for every week of the grading period. Each class can earn two stars a week. One color of star is earned if students return or renew all books (absent students are not counted). Another colored star is earned for using the library well and quietly. At the end of each grading period, count up the total number of stars, and the class with the most stars earns an ice cream party. It seems to be more fair if the grades are divided up by primary and intermediate. Ten to fifteen minutes is plenty of time to swoop into a classroom, scoop out chocolate chip ice cream cones for everyone, give congratulations, and be gone. Students are left with a sense of satisfaction and the competition works well to help get books back on time.

Notes
1. Dahlgren, J. *Preventative Discipline: Tools for Tomorrow, Not Just Theory for Thought.* Coeur d' Alene, ID: Education Development Center, 1996.

REFOCUS FORM
(PRIMARY)

Time out:_____

Name: _____

Date: _____

What did you do? _____

What did you want? _____

What will you do next time? _____

Can you do it? _____

Do you want to talk to your teacher? Yes _____ No _____

Time in:_____

REFOCUS FORM
(Intermediate)

Start time:_____

Name: _____ Date: _____

Teacher/Issuer: _____ Grade: _____

What was your behavior? _____

What should you have been doing? _____

Why did you choose this behavior? _____

_____

_____

What will you do to be successful next time? _____

Are you ready to go back to class and be successful? Yes _____ No _____

Do you want to talk to your teacher or the counselor? Yes _____ No _____

Finish time:_____

Chapter Four

South Korea – wood

Public Relations

Public relations may be a life or death matter for school library media programs. In this day of tight budgets and limited resources, the need for a strong public relations program is readily apparent. Most librarians are so busy that they do a very haphazard job of public relations. It is essential that a continuing and consistent public relations program be carried out in every school library. It has to be systematically done to be effective. Short-term campaigns are of little value.

What is the most important thing a librarian can do to create good public relations? Give good service. If the library is to have any public relations program, it all has to start with the staff. Excellent service will almost be automatic if good relations exist within the library staff. Library employees who are happy with their work and proud of their library will create a friendly and helpful working atmosphere. They will seldom complain and will cheerfully serve students and faculty.

The head librarian must take the staff into her confidence. Supervisors must always be ready to listen to their staff members. The staff must be kept informed of library affairs, policies, decisions, new regulations, promotions, and similar matters. By doing so, the staff sees working in the library as more than just a job. It is essential that a library "attitude" be fostered. While it is intangible, it is the single most important factor in creating a fine school library. The library really doesn't have much to advertise in public relations if it does not have a unified staff, high in morale.

Keep in mind that non-professionals at the circulation desk are the "face" of the library. Head librarians must see that these employees are responsive people who enjoy meeting and working with students, faculty and staff. The library has only one chance to make a positive first impression and non-professionals are usually the first to meet and serve library patrons. It is very difficult, and sometimes impossible, to erase and replace a negative first impression of a library.

It is a wise librarian who will consistently and personally thank her staff for jobs well done.

Events Helping to Foster Positive Impressions of a Library

It is important that the library delivers what it advertises. Never promise what cannot be produced. If the library advertises three-day service on interlibrary loans but it consistently takes a week to ten days, then there is a loss of credibility. *"Promote what you have, and have what you promote,"* is very basic to a successful public relations program. The following library practices help to foster a positive image:

◆ Schedule annual library orientation tours for the faculty.

◆ Teach library and research skills, collaborating with the faculty whenever possible.

◆ Speed new books and other materials to the shelves. Many librarians choose to display them first but they should not be left on display for an inordinate amount of time. New materials should be highlighted at faculty meetings.

◆ Place suggestion boxes in the library with answers posted on a nearby bulletin board.

Schedule orientation tours of the library for new faculty members to acquaint them with the collection and services.

◆ If the library collects book fines and payments for lost books, care should be taken when there is doubt concerning the borrower's delinquency.

Custodial Staff

Some of the most important people to the library are the members of the custodial staff. Cultivating a good working relationship with the custodians is of utmost importance. In order to have good public relations a library must always be clean and inviting. Besides actively maintaining the library, a custodian who will repaint a wall for you, lift heavy boxes, and help dust library shelves, is a treasure. Personal comments and notes of appreciation for their work in the library is a sure way to make friends. It is a wise librarian who thanks a custodian for a job well done rather than ignoring the opportunity because it is part of the custodial job description. Pass those good reviews for great work along to your administration as well. Publicizing an ill-kept library will defeat public relations efforts. Appearances and first impressions are vital to the success of a library's collection and services, and to any public relations program.

It is imperative to remember that the student is more important than the book. Family situations can put a lost book and its payment out of the student's control. Working off a book fine will give the student a sense of responsibility and closure. It will endear the librarian to the concerned classroom teacher, and it will give the librarian and student a chance to get to know one another better.

Discipline in the Library

A positive approach to discipline is part of the public relations effort. This vital matter must be taken care of effectively if the library is to be successful in establishing a reputation of excellence as a learning center. The public relations efforts of the library will be lost if the library is seen as a place where the disruptive actions of students go unchecked. The library is fortunate indeed if there is a school-wide discipline plan. If the librarian can get away from the image of an enforcement officer, so much the better. This is done by having a carefully thought out discipline plan to follow.

Discipline must be taken care of consistently before public relations efforts are successful. Certainly, the library cannot be used as a place where teachers send disruptive students or students who are required to finish classwork on their own time. This turns the library into a punitive area and forever more it will be seen by students in a negative light. Students should view the library as an exciting place to be; a place of reading, research, resources, professional help, and a warm and friendly learning atmosphere. A positive approach to discipline will make this possible, and it is a very important part of the public relations effort.

Be proactive and convey the idea to teachers that the library's importance as a classroom should not be diminished by using it for a disciplinary area.

Other Public Relations Ideas

It is a wise librarian who takes advantage of the publicity generated during National Library Week or Children's Book Week. Numerous library posters, mobiles, and bookmarks are available at a nominal cost. It is important for libraries to promote their programs with such celebratory events.

Bookfairs conducted during back to school night or during parent-teacher conferences, are an excellent means for luring parents to the library. What better way for parents to meet their children's librarian? It is a perfect opportunity for the librarian to be seen in her role of linking children and books.

There are many aspects to a library's public relations. It is vital to remember that public relations must be a process, involving everything from a patron's first impression to large, well-publicized events.

Public Relations and Students: *The Most Important Library Patrons of All*

The goal of any public relations program is to ultimately benefit the students of the school. If students see the school library as an important part of their school day, then the library has succeeded in its public relations efforts. Students are not a hard-sell. They are certainly the most spontaneous and yet appreciative patrons of the library. They need only a smile to feel welcome; someone to listen to them to feel important; someone who is interested in them to feel accepted. Such a school library (librarian) should get a prize for public relation efforts.

How to Become a Student-Oriented Library

The following are some worthwhile procedures to capture students' interest in the library:

1. Talk to students. Listen to their opinions on what materials the library should order. This is the finest way to develop a viable, current collection which will reflect students' interests. Money spent on student-requested materials is effectively spent—the materials will be used. Guiding students to finer literature can only take place after they have developed a love for reading in their own right.

2. If the school librarian discovers she does not have the time to work with students, then a reexamination of priorities is in order. It is imperative that school librarians know students by name and take the time to communicate with them. This is the very foundation of any public relations program. How else will the library's objectives and goals be accomplished if the librarian does not work with both groups and individual students?

3. Students must be led to develop library research skills. They will seldom involve themselves in research projects. These skills have lifelong value and it is imperative that students be taught how to use a library effectively. This should be a joint effort between classroom teachers and the librarian. Thus, the librarian must make every effort to encourage teachers to assign research projects at every grade level and bring their classes to the library. It is a truism that library-oriented teachers are the diamonds of every school.

4. An effective school librarian is often out of the library, promoting the library and its services throughout the school and possibly the community. Any public relation effort must include the willingness of the librarian to attend departmental faculty meetings; meet with individual faculty members; visit classrooms and do whatever has been planned to publicize the library and help patrons use it effectively.

Public Relations With Teachers and Administrators

It is vital that the school librarian work closely with the teachers and administrators of the school. It is understood by all school librarians that the best way to increase the number of students using the library is to sell classroom teachers on the value of assigning their students library projects and/or bringing their classes to the library. A librarian who is willing to fill a cart with library materials and teach library skills in classrooms has a very active public relations program going.

How to Win Faculty Support

Some of the following suggestions may work for you:

1. Use faculty as subject specialists. Ask them to assist in building a current and balanced collection in their subject area or other areas of interest that they will be teaching. Usually it is best to start with the collection where it is and ask their advice concerning materials to be purchased. Always route catalogs and advertisements to them and ask them to prioritize materials that are of interest. This is an effective way to build a vibrant collection as faculty will use what they order, or at least tend to. It is certainly more cost-effective than the librarian making all of the purchasing decisions. The process is complimentary to faculty members and will usually build an atmosphere of exchange and interaction with the library.

2. As discussed elsewhere in this handbook, offer faculty help in the process of creating curriculum, and using the library and its resources to help develop a subject area. If desired, team-teaching a subject or unit with the classroom teacher is an excellent method of instruction and is being done successfully in many schools. There are obvious benefits to the library and its programs with this dual approach to classroom instruction.

3. Maintain a faculty folder in the library for each of the school's faculty members. In the folder, list the member's subject areas and interests. A running summary of the member's preferences, what has been done to promote the library and its services with this individual, and what can be done is invaluable in establishing an effective working relationship with the faculty.

4. Assist the faculty in compiling bibliographic lists of available library materials for specific subject areas being taught in the classroom. Pull the materials when needed and place them on a cart for use in the classroom or library.

5. Publish a newsletter on a monthly basis for faculty and administration. Within the letter, list recently acquired materials and equipment for faculty preview, library news, accomplishments of faculty and classes throughout the school, or community news applicable to the school.

6. Ask various classrooms to present a program or project in the library for other classes in the school to attend.

7. Each month feature a single faculty member or administrator in the library. Include pictures, hobbies, favorite books, and accomplishments. Contact the faculty member for help in accumulating materials for this special area. This is the library's biography of the month.

8. Develop a professional reading center in the library for faculty and administration. Current books, periodicals, and educational media on the curricula taught in the school and the subject specialties of the faculty, is an excellent public relations tool.

9. Meet with all first-year teachers for an in-depth tour of the library and explanation of its services for students and faculty.

10. Sponsor after-school workshops to acquaint faculty with educational media, audiovisual equipment, production materials, etc.

11. Host breakfasts or cookies and punch get togethers for faculty, administration and staff in the library periodically throughout the year.

12. If possible, order personal books for faculty members and administrators at library discount rates.

13. Take student, faculty and administrator opinion polls on the library. Place a suggestion box in the hall for faculty and students with a nearby bulletin board with posted responses to suggestions.

14. Set up district-wide meetings with other school librarians to share ideas for supporting teachers.

15. Help teachers find applicable grant sources.

16. Always attend faculty and staff meetings and be an active participant.

17. Meet with each individual teacher at least twice a year for a private conversation concerning their instructional needs and interests.

18. Remember teachers and administrators on their birthdays with a bookmark, card, or small gift.

These are just a few suggestions. Many may not work for you, but others will. The authors are sure you will think of other effective public relations tools for your school library. Your positive mind-set will lead to success.

The Community and Public Relations

All efforts involving the community will pay huge dividends for a school library in terms of increased community support. Making available the library's collection and services to the community, or having community organizations and patrons come to the library, is one of the finest ways to promote the library and its programs.

Effective Steps for Community Involvement

1. Develop and keep a list of community members who are willing to volunteer time and expertise to the school, be it in the library or classroom.

2. Develop a file of community experts who are willing to present programs in their areas of expertise for students, faculty, and community members, i.e., various civic clubs, individual farmers, artists, medical doctors, mechanics, etc.

3. Open the library and its facilities for community use in the evenings and weekends if this a library objective. Such action would need approval by the school and/or district administrators.

4. Develop a file of community organizations, businesses, and individuals who may be contacted for library and school fund-raising purposes. The librarian should serve as the school's contact person with these organizations that are outside of the educational community.

5. If no other entity is involved, the school library should become the community's depository center for local history, ethnological collections of the past and present for the community, and current community status. This would need support of the district, the school, and the community.

Chapter Five

Principals & Librarians

China – papier maché

One of the most vital skills to be acquired by elementary or secondary students during their educational experience is that of achieving library competency. Knowing how to effectively use a library is the foundation of education and lifelong learning. Information and its related services are a major product for the United States. A district or school that does not include the library and its instructional programs throughout the curriculum is outdated and perpetuating a disservice to students who are now facing vocational and educational decisions.

What determines whether or not a library plays an essential and viable role in students' education? Is it the professional training, philosophy, or work ethic of the school librarian? Is it the use and support of the library's collection and facilities by the faculty? Is it student use of the library? As important as these factors are, research has shown that the single most important factor determining the role of the library in a school is "whether or not the school principal is aware of and sympathetic to it"[1]

Unfortunately, effective library instruction and library services for students are often dependent upon personalities and working relationships between librarians and the principal of the school. Successful working relationships between the principal and the librarian usually result in the library and its instructional programs being an integral part of the school's total educational process. Too frequently, however, library instruction and school libraries have an insignificant role in a student's education. Often the librarian is partially at fault, sometimes the administrator. Both need to work together to establish an effective library program for faculty and students. Without this working relationship, students lose a vital part of their education.

> Never contact the principal concerning a library problem without having thought of some possible solutions.

Basic Rules for Working With School Administrators

The following are some basic rules which every librarian should incorporate into her relationship with school administrators.[2] It is worthwhile for both the principal and the librarian to be aware of them.

✍ It is very important to contact the administrator frequently when there are positive aspects of the library's program to show and tell them. Invite them to come to the library often and acquaint them with the many valuable services and accomplishments of the library. The librarian should be viewed as a positive source of information.3

✍ Principals seldom have strong library backgrounds. They are usually former classroom teachers, not librarians. The best thing a school librarian can do when faced with a library problem that needs the principal's help is to have several possible solutions in mind. This creates two positive situations. One, the principal appreciates a professional's input and is not left "hanging alone." Two, library problems are often unique to the library and need a "library" perspective to solve them. Weeding the collection and volunteer help in the library are examples that come to mind.

✍ Keep the principal informed so she is always knowledgeable concerning the library and its programs. Setting up an annual professional goals conference for the library and the librarian is imperative. (See the sample professional growth plan at the end of this chapter.) In districts where the principals read weekly classroom teacher lesson plans, the principal should do the same for the librarian's flexible scheduling, library skills classes and classroom curricula tie-ins.

✍ Ask for advice in those situations where there is no clear policy.

✍ Establish the librarian and the library as an indispensable cog in the school's educational picture. The following are some proven methods that will contribute to this goal.

> **Teach library skills to students.** Be willing to do so in the classrooms if necessary. Have librarian, will travel.
>
> **Involve students in building the library's collection**. Ask for their input in book selection. The materials they request will be heavily used.
>
> **Include faculty and administration whenever possible in library events, programs, and services**.
>
> **Work closely with faculty to order library materials in their subject areas and other areas of interest.** Why other areas of interest? Because faculty will often teach or refer to these interests in their classrooms. This is "strength teaching," and it should always be encouraged.
>
> **Use faculty as subject area specialists and as resource people whenever possible.**
>
> **The librarian should be active in curriculum decision making throughout the school**, both as to (1), supporting curricula in the school with library resources and (2), helping to relate and teach curricula with interested faculty members.
>
> **Be familiar with school policy**, i.e., the school's approach to discipline, educational mission, statement of philosophy, etc.
>
> **Be personally visible.** Attend faculty meetings, conferences, and workshops. Be an active participant in the educational process.
>
> **If possible, provide library services to the community in which the school is located.**

Problems can arise between administrators and librarians. Instead of educators, administrators often view librarians as technical specialists, who seem insensitive towards the administrator's job of achieving scholastic and financial balance throughout the school and across the curriculum. Some librarians are viewed as narrowly focused kingdom-builders and libraries themselves as fiscal bottomless pits. Far too often the most frequent communication between the librarian and school principal concerns the needs of the library or a library problem.

Other problem areas are censorship confrontations in which principals order librarians to remove books from shelves or delete passages and illustrations to accommodate complaints from a parent, patron, or perhaps a school board member. Having a censorship policy in place will help alleviate this problem.

Funding is always a concern. Frequently, the library is targeted for budget and staff cuts.

Through all of this, it must be remembered that principals are usually former classroom teachers, not former librarians. They are usually more knowledgeable concerning teaching and classroom needs than in having a working knowledge of the functions and needs of a library. Many librarians become frustrated when they cannot act according to their professional knowledge and standards, under limitations placed upon them

> Problems between principals and librarians generally fall into two categories—censorship and funding.

by their school principals. These problems stem from the fact that often school principals lack an understanding of the vital role a library has in the educational process.

Why is there a communication gap between librarians and principals? In almost every instance, the course work required for school administrators does not include training in the importance of the library's role in society and in the school's curriculum. This lack of library training in educational administration can have a devastating impact on a library's collection, informational services, and ultimately, students' education.

How to remedy these situations? The school librarian must share in the responsibility of a principal's administrative myopia. That is, in the absence of a formal education about the library's importance and operation, the school librarian must not miss any opportunity to demonstrate the value of library instruction and the library itself in practical application. If a library course is not included in an educational administration curriculum, librarians need to ask for the necessary time to meet with such classes as guest speakers or specialists, and provide necessary library instruction and exposure. Something is far better than nothing. Well-organized presentations need not be extensive; a class period or two can be of significant value to future administrators to acquaint them with the importance of having an active library program in their schools. Helping each school administrator to become aware of the role of libraries in the educational process can benefit hundreds, if not thousands of students. A positive working relationship between principals and librarians must be a reality in every school.

Notes

1. Carlson, R.O. *Changing Processes in Public Schools.* Eugene, OR: Eugene Center for Advanced Study of Educational Administration. University of Oregon. 1965.

2. Weisburg, H.K. and Ruth Toor. "The Administrator and You: Enhancing Your Image." *The School Librarian's Workshop,* (January, 1988).

3. Howland, P. "Sure Fire LMC Reports." *School Library Journal.* 26, (1979). p.126.

Sample Forms and Reports

The three forms selected for reproduction on the next several pages can provide support for a meaningful, productive relationship between librarian and principal.

Professional Growth Plan Form: This example of a professional growth plan is to be used by school librarians and principals in their annual professional growth interview. This important process has been in existence for years with the principal and faculty members. Librarians must be included in professional growth conferences.

Substitute Librarian Form: Second, there is a form to be used when a substitute librarian is called and the regularly assigned librarian cannot be in attendance. Using this form will assure a smooth and effective transition for the students and the faculty of the school.

Monthly Media Report: This report on the library's activities is sent to faculty and administration. Copies should be filed for future reference by the librarian.

Professional Growth Plan Form

Between Librarians and Principals

* GOAL STATEMENT (What is desired?)
The focus of your goal statement should be one of the four major areas in which teacher growth and competence are assessed (instruction, classroom procedures, interpersonal skills, or professional standards). See your handbook, "Guidelines for the Assessment of Professional Teacher Growth for the Improvement of Instruction."

* Objective Statement(s) (What specifically do you want to do?):

* Activity Statement(s) (How will you reach your objectives?):

* Assessment (How will you know when you reach your objectives?):

* Target Date (When will the objective be completed?):

Jefferson Elementary School
"Creating the Desire for Life-Long Learning"

Chuck Wegner, Principal   *1455 Gwen Drive*
Nada Wehrli, Secretary   *Pocatello, Idaho 83204*
                                                             (208) 232-2914

SUBSTITUTE LIBRARIAN

MEDIA CENTER PROCEDURES

1. School begins: ___*8:35*___

2. Lunch: ___*12:00 - 12:30*___

3. School ends: ___*2:40*___

4. Recess duty: *Tuesday afternoon, 1:50 - 2:00, 5th grade end of building, top of hill*

5. Get help from: *Shirley Edwards, Library Assistant, Chuck Wegner, Principal*

6. Lesson plans and class schedule: *End of counter near check out computer*

7. Location of books to read aloud: *Bottom shelf of counter or blue table by willow chair*

8. Location of library skills materials: *Blue table or 3rd shelf down in wardrobe*

9. Opening routine: ★*Be at the stage as students come in, to insure order* ★*Students enter & sit in the same order they are lined up in* ★*Top step fills first* ★*K-1 sits on all 3 steps in middle section* ★*2-6 sit on top & bottom steps clear across stage with middle step for feet* ★*read list of overdue books marking those who are absent (A), renewing ()K), or have forgotten books (√)* ★*Teach library skills &/or story (see lesson plans)* ★*Dismiss by colors being worn, types of shoes, eye color, etc.* ★*K-1 sit at tables if book is missing* ★*2-6 sit at tables if both books are missing* ★*No moving around for these students*

10. Rules: ★*Whisper/no running* ★*Get books quickly & quietly then sit & read* ★*They are expected to sit in one spot & read!* ★*Boat - 2 people, all grades* ★*Train - K-1 two per car & 2-6 one per car* ★*Bean bags - 1 or 2 per bag* ★*Willow chair - 1 or 2 depending on size*

11. Rewards: *Each class can earn a red star if all books are returned or renewed and a blue star if the library is used quietly and well.*

12. Bathroom procedure: *Ask classroom teacher or dismiss one at a time. Hold their books until they return.*

13. In case of emergency: *Use the beige phone in the workroom to call the office.*

14. Fire drill: *Students exit the same way they came into the library and leave the building by their regular exit with no talking.*

MONTHLY MEDIA REPORT　　　　　　　　　DATE:

CIRCULATION:
BOOKS:
MAGAZINES:

MEDIA CENTER USE BY CLASSES:
LAB USE BY CLASSES:

BUDGET BALANCE:
ACQUISITIONS:
DISCARDS:
NUMBER OF BOOKS IN INVENTORY:

NO. OF AV ITEMS CIRCULATED FROM DISTRICT:

COMMENTS:
　　　Mrs. Merkley and I are working closely together…
　　　I taught 9th grade students from Mr. Mortimer's class…
　　　Our camcorder was dropped…

Jefferson Elementary
Dewey Collection Statistics

Today's Date: Nov. 03, 1998

Range	Total Circs		Yearly Circs		Monthly Circs		Collection	
001-099	364	(00.5%)	7	(00.1%)	6	(00.2%)	37	(00.3%)
100-199	200	(00.3%)	7	(00.1%)	3	(00.1%)	37	(00.3%)
200-299	168	(00.2%)	13	(00.2%)	10	(00.3%)	37	(00.3%)
300-399	2,942	(04.5%)	78	(01.4%)	43	(01.4%)	480	(03.9%)
400-499	620	(00.9%)	14	(00.2%)	7	(00.2%)	74	(00.6%)
500-599	11,015	(17.0%)	314	(05.8%)	156	(05.4%)	985	(08.0%)
600-699	3,535	(05.4%)	87	(01.6%)	40	(01.3%)	421	(03.4%)
700-799	5,561	(08.6%)	206	(03.8%)	126	(04.3%)	384	(03.1%)
800-899	2,255	(03.4%)	69	(01.2%)	40	(01.3%)	272	(02.2%)
900-999	5,187	(08.0%)	80	(01.4%)	51	(01.7%)	705	(05.7%)
AV	1,391	02.1%)	28	(00.5%)	14	(00.4%)	467	(03.8%)
BIO	58	(00.0%)	17	(00.3%)	14	(00.4%)	203	(01.6%)
E	23,994	(37.2%)	846	(15.6%)	411	(14.3%)	2,140	(17.4%)
F	13,952	(21.6%)	373	(06.9%)	193	(06.7%)	1,720	(14.0%)
FIC	611	(00.9%)	223	(04.1%)	126	(04.3%)	164	(01.3%)
MAG	2,073	(03.2%)	315	(05.8%)	179	(06.2%)	437	(03.5%)
OTH	3,962	(06.1%)	63	(01.1%)	39	(01.3%)	692	(05.6%)
PB	35,031	(054.3%)	2,624	(48.6%)	1,395	(48.5%)	2,183	(17.7%)
REF	1,139	(01.7%)	6	(00.1%)	6	(00.2%)	298	(02.4%)
TEM	48	(00.0%)	10	(00.1%)	7	(00.2%)	2	(00.0%)
TS	430	(00.6%)	11	(00.2%)	7	(00.2%)	533	(04.3%)
	114,536		5,391		2,873		12,271	

Chapter Six

Two Professionals in Every Classroom

Chile – wood

Every student must develop at least an entry-level capability in literacy and informational access skills in order to survive in today's information-age world.[1] Thankfully, classroom teachers do not have to face this challenge alone. While teachers have always had the library's book, periodical, and media collections to supplement their curricula, today there is an exciting program, predominate in library literature, which will specifically help classroom teachers develop curricula in any subject area. It involves the librarian working with individual classroom teachers in the design and implementation of curricula. In this program, the librarian contributes her expertise in library resources and services, and the classroom teacher develops and guides the program towards student achievement.

Curricula designed through the dual efforts of a faculty member and a librarian will include both the subject content and skills to be mastered by the students, as well as the library research and informational skills needed by the students to complete the unit. Personally involving students in research and processing skills in any subject area is a proven method of mastering content. Also, using library skills to learn a subject area is one of the finest ways to teach students how to effectively use a library and process information. This has long-term value as it enables students to make informed choices throughout their lives. Both goals are met when teachers and librarians team together to design curricula for student learning. Many librarians refer to this process as flexible scheduling.

The literature and service background of a certified school librarian should be utilized in every classroom's curricula. Library resources and the expertise of the librarian should be an integral part of the instructional program. The librarian can help develop the curriculum and assist in teaching it, if the classroom teacher so desires. Often, the librarian is able to use library funds to purchase materials to support the curricula and build the library's collection in a given subject area. This team approach would reflect "on the spot" needs of students with the immediate resources that are available. It would supplement commercially developed programs, which are being marketed nationally, and personalize the curricula in each school to local area needs and resources. Who are the ultimate benefactors? The students are, and that is what the school library is all about.

School librarians have long enjoyed frequent student use of the library largely because of library-oriented faculty members who bring their classes for assignments, and projects. Librarians realize that it is the classroom teachers who largely determine how often students use library facilities and services. Efforts to increase student use of library resources must be centered on the faculty in order to achieve any large degree of success. What better way to involve the faculty than teaming to design curricula?

The following are examples of units at the elementary and secondary levels. They were designed and taught by Mary Jo Pearson, an elementary teacher in Mackay, Idaho, and Alice Crockett, a librarian, at Skyline High School, Idaho Falls, Idaho.

An Elementary School Experience

In the rural community of Mackay, Idaho, an elementary teacher started a literature-based thematic unit on birds by reading aloud E .B. White's, *The Trumpet of the*

Two professionals are involved in creating classroom curricula; the teacher and the librarian.

Becoming involved in planning is a logical step because the librarian is already selecting and contributing materials for units of study.

Efforts to increase student use of library resources must be centered on the faculty.

Swan. The students enjoyed the book and were eager to learn more about birds. The librarian gathered resources, and shared stories, poems, and informational books, joining with the teacher in building background and motivating students. After building background knowledge, students chose their own favorite birds on which to study and report. The librarian and classroom teacher joined together to aid students in topic selection and research during flexibly scheduled library times. Students were actively involved in locating facts and transferring them to index cards for later reference. Every day, during writing workshops in the classroom, students worked on bird reports, referring to their fact cards. The librarian guided students in developing a title page for their reports and the students painted pictures of birds for their report covers as an art project.

Meanwhile, the classroom was being transformed into an aviary of sorts through artwork, completed bird projects, musical games, songs, and bird calls. Resources flowed between the library and the classroom as needed. Students studied John Audubon and his paintings and then did their own watercolors. They patterned themselves after Sam Beaver, the young boy in White's, *The Trumpet of the Swan,* as they observed and recorded their observations of birds feeding at simple handmade feeders at home. Students brought their observations to math classes and the results were graphed. Creative movement in physical education classes was performed as if the students were "birds" flying in new formations. In music, students participated in songs and musical games centered around birds. Humanities themes prevalent in E.B. White's story were explored, such as loyalty, responsibility, love, and family values. Louis, the trumpeter swan and main character in the book, flew from Western Canada to Montana, and then to Boston. A map in the media center allowed students to track his travels with the aid of map keys.

The culminating experience was a Spirit Day Assembly entitled "Birds Do the Strangest Things," with students sharing artwork, poetry, musical games, riddles, and bird calls with the rest of the student body. The assembly took place in the school library and was videotaped by the librarian.

Language arts and other subject areas were integrated into a meaningful unit of study. This was accomplished through the collaborative efforts of the classroom teacher and school librarian designing and teaching a curriculum on birds. The entire student body benefited from this effort, and it was a synoptic teaching experience for this class in Mackay, Idaho.

A High School Experience

A second example involved a high school class in Idaho Falls, Idaho. The theme was human solitude. Many young adult books and articles have solitude, loneliness, and isolation as their theme. All young adults have these emotions and senses pulsing in their lives. The students want to be individuals, yet they also want to be part of the whole. They are amazed to find out that their fears, misgivings, and intuitions are universal; that they can be talked about and they have been written about in novels, short stories, plays, poetry, magazine and journal articles.

The class met the first day in the library. A "solitude" reading list consisting of novels, short stories, poems, and articles, available in the media center, was handed out to each student. A discussion with the students by the teacher and librarian opened up the dimension of the state or emotions of solitude: being alone, feelings of loneliness, isolation, and the positive and negative need for others. Each student checked out at least one reading from the list and was responsible for sharing it with the class. Students kept a journal of responses and reactions to what they read, what their peers reported, and the audiovisual materials available on the subject from the library.

Students, depending upon their special interests, brought to class real life instances and examples of solitude as found in society, nature, politics, and their own

Helping publish booklets of student poetry and writings dealing with solitude would extend this project.

personal lives. When possible, the class met two class periods each week in the media center to research books, periodicals, CDs and telecommunications for real life instances. As a culminating activity, the media center hosted a forum where students presented their reports and findings. The outcome? Collaboration between the librarian and classroom teacher enabled students to research and report upon the importance of solitude in each of their lives.

Extending the Library's Reach

Three decades of library research have documented the isolation of the school library in schools' instructional programs.[2] Up until now, the library has been relied on for information and materials for classroom support. Seldom have librarians been involved with faculty in the actual design of instruction. *Times are changing!*

Resources, research, and the informational expertise of a professional librarian are all available to assist students in mastering content. The librarian is totally familiar with the curriculum, as she helped design it. The benefits are obvious to all concerned.

Two other crucial roles of the library need to be mentioned. First, the school library needs to develop or have a center which will assist in the professional growth of the faculty. The center should have professional journals, books, and cross-curriculum materials, as well as materials on given subject areas. There are numerous resources on flexible scheduling, both in theory and practical application, and the more material that can be made available to faculty, the more students will benefit. Providing professional literature for faculty is a definite responsibility of every school librarian. Since principals are the overseers of professional growth in the school, they are an invaluable resource in suggesting purchases for the faculty collection.

Second, the librarian should be aware of outside agencies and citizens who can and are willing to help the school educate children. Businesses, universities, parent-teacher organizations, and individuals, provide tremendous support that extends and embellishes the library and school. Librarians should acquaint themselves with what is available and become the contact person between such organizations and the faculty.

Flexible Scheduling

Michael Bell and Herman Trotten found in their study that schools were more effective academically when librarians were actively working with faculty in designing and implementing instruction.[3] The use of library resources and media to help achieve learner objectives has proven to be far more effective than traditional classroom textbook teaching. Textbook oriented teachers, in any subject area, are seldom a factor in motivating students to use the library as part of the curriculum. Lowell Olson concluded in a 1983 study that those students "corralled by the textbook" find little real need to use the library.[4]

Flexible scheduling gives students a chance to have access to the library and its materials at all times of the school day. It also gives teachers the opportunity to schedule the library for their classes whenever the need arises rather than just once a week. The library becomes a resource area for reading books and finding materials which are not available in the classroom.

How to start? Possibly with the librarian talking with an active library-using teacher about more library cross-curriculum involvement. Possibly by discussing the program in a faculty or departmental head meeting. Possibly with a two-on-one brainstorming session between the principal, a faculty member, and the librarian.

Teachers need to be sold on cross-curriculum teaching of library skills. The more the librarian works with classroom faculty, the more ideas will develop for cross-curriculum teaching. When teachers see that library skills units are essential to classroom lessons, and students realize that there is a definite purpose for coming to the library,

Rather than having faculty bring their classes to the library for supplemental materials, the library becomes an area of instruction.

The more involvement the librarian has with the community in which the school resides, the better the school is; and the librarian is seen as an indispensable cog in the education of children.

With flexible scheduling, the library becomes the focal point of learning in the school.

Most important, teachers and librarians will find that the curricula of the classroom will drive what library skills will be taught and when, not the other way around.[5]

then flexible scheduling benefits are obvious. While the librarian must be certain that all library skills are taught, flexible scheduling permits them to be taught when they relate to classroom assignments and activities. It is not even too important who teaches these skills. It can be the librarian, classroom teacher, or by co-teaching. Teachers will appreciate this flexibility.

Faculty have real concerns about giving up part of their planning time to initiate flexible scheduling with the librarian. Also, they often want to know if they must be personally present when the librarian is presenting. Once the cross-curriculum scheduling has been worked out, faculty will find that it will usually cover several classroom periods and the planning time will be made up. Also, once done, it needs only updating to be used in the future. Whether or not the librarian wishes to have the classroom teacher assist would depend upon the curricula. These teacher concerns are real but they have been successfully worked out in untold numbers of schools and the benefits to students make the efforts very worthwhile.

Initially, not all faculty in a school will want the librarian to be involved in curriculum design. However, there are those who will. The results of librarian/faculty teamwork in curriculum design have been well substantiated.[7] The results are soon apparent to non-participating faculty members. With the increased supporters, materials and drive, the program will accelerate on its own, as will student achievement.

> When a teacher requests materials for a unit of study, go the extra step and offer to dovetail a library skills class that will go along with the subject.

Notes

1. Glasser, W. *The Quality School Teacher.* New York: HarperCollins, 1993.

2. Naylor, A. P. and Jenkins, K. D. "An investigation of principals' perceptions of library media specialists' performance evaluation terminology." *School Library Media Quarterly,* 16, (1988). p. 234-43.

3. Bell, M. and Trotten, H. L. "School climate factors related to degrees of cooperation between public elementary school teachers and school library media specialists." *The Library Quarterly,* (1991). 61, p. 302-309.

4. Olson, L. E. Unassailable truth? A look at the concept of school library media specialists as teachers. School Library Media Quarterly, 12, (1983). p. 44-57.

5. Ohlrich, I. B. "Flexible Scheduling: The Dream vs. Reality." *School Library Journal.* (May, 1992). p.35-38.

6. "Convincing teachers. The key to flexible scheduling." *School Librarian's Workshop.* (May, 1993). p. 9-10.

7. Op Cit., Bell and Trotten.

Chapter Seven

The Faculty–Library Committee

Mexico (Tarahumara) –wood

The one indispensable organization in any library is the faculty–library committee. The librarian should make sure that such a committee is appointed or elected at the beginning of every school year. Don't leave home without it. The committee should be small with one or two faculty members, an administrator, the librarian, and perhaps a member of the community. This committee performs an invaluable service for the entire school as well as the library. The committee becomes a "sounding board" for the community, a means of communication for ethnic minorities, special events, censorship problems, and other matters relating directly to the library.

It meets, functions, and reports back to its constituencies only as an advisory body. Decisions are then made by the faculty, administration or librarian, depending on the issue. The committee can study library needs, resources, services, and programs. Most important, it is the main tool to be used in censorship problems. For this function alone, the committee is an absolute necessity. This is the committee which uses the district-wide written library acquisitions policy to guide library purchasing of materials for the collection and library services. Using this document, the committee is able to review questionable materials which are of concern to faculty members or members of the community. The committee is often able to make a final decision, if empowered by the school to do so, whether or not the materials in question should be included in the library's collection or used in the classroom. It is vital that a committee be used in the process rather than the lone voice of the principal or librarian.

It must always be kept in mind that the faculty/library committee functions as only an advisory committee.

Other committee responsibilities can include:

- Funding needed beyond the library's budget for such things as physical plant, capital expenditures, etc., (carpeting, air conditioning, furniture).

- The library's role in the automation of the school and Internet use, possibly networking with classrooms, the district and other libraries.

- The involvement, if any, of the school library facilities and services with the local community.

- Library public relations programs.

- Evaluation of the library's role in the school's educational mission.

- Policies on accepting gifts and donations to the library.

- Promoting student, faculty, and community use of the library's collection and services.

The list can go on and on. However, if the committee is used for nothing more than censorship issues and selection review, it will be invaluable. The faculty–library advisory committee is a very effective voice for the library and is heard more readily, in many instances, than that of the librarian. It has been found that it is one of the most effective tools that a library can have to help meet the many opportunities and problems that every library experiences. Everyone benefits.

If you are going to have a faculty/library committee, use it—constantly!

Personal Experiences With Faculty/Library Committees

Case A

At a mid-sized Western elementary school, the faculty-library committee was an incredible attribute to the library and the entire school was aware of its influence. The librarian was never the lone voice in trying to fulfill the library's mission throughout the year. When budget time came around each fall for the following year, the library's budget was submitted to the administration under the signature of the committee chairperson, members, and librarian. Censorship incidents, budgets, working with local community organizations, public relations, promoting the library's collection and services to the school as well as the community, were all responsibilities dealt with by the committee. At the same time, the committee was aware that it was an advisory board to the school library, and it never tried to usurp the librarian's role. The faculty-library committee was viewed throughout the school as one of the most effective and respected committees.

Case B

Having had such a positive experience with a faculty-library committee at the elementary school level, the librarian tried to establish such a committee at a community college library which she directed. She was informed by administration that such a committee already existed and was made up of departmental chairpersons of the various divisions on campus. The chairs met weekly and thus a continuous process was in place.

After numerous attempts to involve the committee in library concerns, the librarian found that the departmental chairs were far too involved in their own divisions and responsibilities to lend much time or expertise to a library committee. The college administration felt comfortable with the library committee as it was and felt no need to disband it and create a new faculty-library committee.

The bottom line was that the library was never served effectively by the committee and therefore, the students never enjoyed the benefits of an advisory committee actively serving their needs at the library.

Examples of Involving a Faculty–Library Committee

A Censorship Incident

The parents of a junior-high-age girl were concerned that a classroom teacher had discussed the book, *Go Ask Alice*. The teacher had elected not to read the book to the class nor obtain the several copies necessary for class members to read it. However, she did feel the book would be of value if students read and discussed it with their parents at home. Of course, every student wanted a copy of the book to see why the teacher asked them to include parental direction.

The young girl obtained a copy of the book, read parts of it to her mother, and both parents came to the school feeling the book to be inappropriate reading material. Interestingly enough, the principal referred them to the librarian rather than the classroom teacher since the school had a faculty-library committee. The librarian welcomed the parents to the library and immediately took the time to discuss the book with them. A complaint form was given to the parents necessitating that the parents read the book in its entirety.

They did so, filled out the complaint form, and the case was forwarded to the committee. Upon deliberation, the committee ruled that the book would remain accessible to students in the school library. After having read the complete book and knowing of the committee's decision, the parents agreed there was value to retaining the book in the collection.

The process had been followed. The committee functioned as was intended. The complaint was handled professionally, courteously, and both the school and parents were better for the experience. A letter was written, co-signed by both the principal and the librarian, thanking the parents for their concern and involvement.

A Fundraising Dinner

A faculty–library committee started an annual homemade chili, cinnamon roll evening dinner at the school lunch room to be attended by families having children in the school. The local PTA was contacted to advertise the dinner, arrange for the food, and to host the event. All teachers, administrators, and board members were invited to attend. Expenses for the first dinner were provided from PTA funds, which were repaid by donations at the conclusion of the dinner. Since then, the dinner has been provided by the children's parents and has been self-funding and very profitable. Minimal charges per family raised enough money for special library projects throughout the year.

The real success of the venture was the community involvement and interaction with the school by local families. The event is now an annual school tradition, always well attended. It affords an opportunity for parents to socialize with faculty, administrators and board members of the school and district while getting to tour the library and other school facilities. Parents become acquainted with the school's programs and needs.

The event has been held for the past 23 years and is still going strong. It has proved to be a marvelous public relations program, helping to weld the school with its community.

Faculty Support for the Library

In every school there are those faculty members who seldom use the library; do not assign their students library projects; seldom, if ever, invite the librarian to visit or teach in their classrooms; and, in all, do not include the library in the education of their students.

When invited to become a member of a functioning faculty-library committee, such faculty members often become active supporters and users of the library. It happens more often than not. Reluctant faculty are targeted by the committee for membership for a particular school year or at least, a few months of the year. The first-hand exposure to the library's role in the education of the students will often change the attitude of the most hardened faculty member.

This was found to be a valuable by-product of the faculty-library committee. It was never a single occurrence but happened repeatedly over the years, much to the amazement of other faculty. The bottom line is that many students benefit from the transformation.

Chapter Eight

Censorship

Hawaii – wood

Criticism is not necessarily censorship. Any person or group has a right to discuss with the librarian reasons for purchasing or not purchasing library materials. Only when someone or some group seeks to have library materials banned, removed from the shelves, or restricted in use, is that person assuming the role of a censor. Librarians can respect and work with any parent who cares enough to oversee their child's reading, but no parent has the right to withhold a book from other children. Once the door to censorship is opened, it is not easy to close.

To demand that a book be banned, we must be willing to award other people the right to make similar demands. If every person or group were given the privilege to remove library materials from the shelves, which were not to their personal liking, libraries would soon have no materials left. It is when adults see themselves as the protectors of innocent children that they lose sight of other people's rights. They don't seem to realize the implications of saying, "No one else should look at this book because I've decided that it is harmful to children."

> There are movements today to ban whole subject areas from the library, not just individual books.

Responding to Requests for Restriction or Removal

Librarians may want to suggest the following to parents or guardians who wish to have library materials restricted or removed from circulation:

- Don't condemn any book until it has been read in its entirety. Titles can be misleading. Also, librarians will need to know what part(s) of the book are objectionable.

- If a teacher is using a book which a parent objects to, do not register a formal complaint until the teacher has been spoken to and it has been determined exactly how the book is being used. Some controversial books can be effectively used in classroom instruction and discussions.

- If a parent opposes the ideas in a book that their child is reading or a teacher is using for instruction, suggest to the parent they take the opportunity to discuss with their child the reasons they oppose the book. One object of education is to enable children to think for themselves concerning controversial materials and situations. What is needed is the skill to sift the wheat from the chaff in life. Dealing with controversial materials can help develop life-long skills of discernment.

> Censorship grows out of fear, and there is a tremendous amount of fear on the part of some parents as they relate to their children's schooling.

Recommended Procedures for Handling a Challenge

- The school librarian cannot handle censorship alone. The best thing a school faculty can do is have a library–faculty committee. This group should consist of the librarian, at least two faculty members, an administrator, and possibly a concerned parent. It can be an invaluable asset to the school and library.

- This group functions as an advisory board. A librarian who uses a faculty committee's suggestions, uses the committee to review censorship requests, and follows the committee's recommendations concerning withdrawing or keeping the materials in question, is well on the way to having a marvelous school year, even if it does include censorship incidents.

- A district-wide library selection policy will help guide the librarian and faculty as they purchase library materials to support the curriculum. Written guidelines will assure consistency in library acquisitions and will become the basis for spending budget monies effectively as well as dealing with censorship problems.

- It is important to have a written complaint form for parents and guardians to use concerning library materials to which they object. The authors recommend a standard form to be used district-wide. Parents who care enough to read the materials and complete a form concerning their objections, are entitled to full efforts and consideration by the librarian. The complaint form is reviewed by the faculty–library committee as a basis for making a decision concerning the materials in question. Thus far, the courts have upheld the vast majority of committee-recommended actions concerning censorship. It is seen as much more effective than censorship decisions made by a single librarian.

Librarians should work graciously with parents who want to oversee their child's reading. Parental criticism of a book is not necessarily censorship. Keep the line of communication open!

Three Additional Kinds of Censorship

There are further censorship concerns. School libraries need only to purchase those items for the collection which support the school's curriculum. Public libraries purchase all types of materials. Both types of libraries have been accused of "non-purchase" censorship. Controversial materials simply are not purchased, thereby avoiding censorship problems. The "non-purchase" philosophy, taken to the extreme, can cause librarians to pass up very fine instructional and worthwhile materials. Achieving a balance in the library's collection is essential. Librarians often ask the faculty–library committee for input on "non-purchase" decisions. After these decisions have been made, school librarians can refer students to public libraries and their broader collections.

Second, while some controversial materials are not removed from the shelves, they are simply altered. Mutilated, might be a better word. Pictures and objectionable statements are cut out or marked over. This is one of the most objectionable forms of censorship. It would be better not to purchase the items in the first place, (non-purchase censorship) than to mutilate them.

A third form of censorship is to "lock-up" library materials. The library has the materials but students must request them specifically in order to access them. They are not found within the library's regular collection. In some extreme cases, these materials are not included on the online or card catalog for circulation. Their collection becomes a library within a library, so to speak.

What can you do if a censorship incident comes your way?

Censorship can be a frightful word to many librarians. It need not be. If the school's faculty/library committee is in place and functioning, librarians have little to fear. Simply acknowledge the concerns of the protesting adult with graciousness and hand them a censorship form to fill out. This alone often separates those people who have never read the book but are simply passing on a complaint from those who are genuinely concerned and have read the materials. Explain that filling out the form is a necessary first step before the faculty–library committee will review the materials. Upon receipt of the form, the committee takes on the problem rather than the librarian. When a committee is in place and is guided by written acquisition and censorship policies, informed and equitable decisions can be made.

If a censorship incident does arise, remain calm. Most incidents come from parents or small groups having little or no community backing. Treat complaints with dignity and courtesy. Handle the complaint under previously established procedures using the faculty–library committee, and the censorship form. Should the complaint be taken further than the committee, the following is advised:

Maintaining a collection of censorship incidents as reported by the media can be a valuable resource in handling local censorship issues.

- Take immediate steps to assure that the full facts surrounding the complaint are known to your administration. Full, written information should be presented giving the nature of the problem or complaint and identifying the sources.

◆ Seek the support of the local press immediately. The freedom to read and the freedom of the press go hand in hand.

◆ Inform local civic organizations of the facts and enlist their support where possible.

◆ Defend the principles of the freedom to read and the professional responsibility of teachers and librarians, rather than the individual book or item that is in question.

◆ The ALA Intellectual Freedom Committee and other appropriate national and state committees concerned with intellectual freedom should be informed of the nature of the problem. Even though each effort at censorship must be met at the local level, there is often value in the support and assistance of agencies outside the area which have no personal involvement. They can often cite parallel cases and suggest methods of meeting an attack.

Aid in cases affecting the use of books in the schools can be obtained from the Commission on Professional Rights and Responsibilities of the National Education Association and the American Library Association's Office of Intellectual Freedom.

The Internet: Unfettered Access for Students?

"The Internet is raising problems, issues and concerns that we've never dealt with before," says Judith Krug, director of the ALA's Office for Intellectual Freedom. She refers to the Library Bill of Rights and the First Amendment in defending unfettered access to the Internet by all Americans, children as well as adults.[1] Many school librarians are caught up in the dilemma as they are supportive of the ALA's endorsement of intellectual freedom and the First Amendment. At the same time, they may feel a moral responsibility to the students, parents and community in which they reside. The root of the controversy is that while there should be no restrictions for adult use of the Internet — What about children? What about school libraries?

The emergence of the Internet has forever changed the way that Americans access information. The "Net" must be included in every school's curriculum. It is essential that students be taught research skills on the Internet the same as they are taught skills using the online catalog, periodical directories, reference works, etc. The problem is that there are real concerns over children accessing sexually explicit materials on the Internet that the library would not include in its collection.

Some Approaches to the Problem

One approach is to turn this problem over to parents. Let parents be responsible for their children's access; a library should access all types of information and have no informational restrictions. This may work for public libraries, but it will hardly do for schools. First, school libraries do not access all types of information, but exist to support the curriculum that is being taught. Secondly, parents are not in classes with their children and have entrusted schools to not only cover the curriculum, but, in most instances, to teach and model moral values. Librarians and teachers feel that the majority of parents would want them to intervene with students when they see sexually oriented materials on the Internet screen.

A second approach is for school classrooms and libraries to use software filters which restrict access to pornographic materials. Whether or not there should be restrictions is the current debate. Filtering software programs are only successful in blocking sexually explicit materials to a point. They cannot block all programmed sites. As the Internet expands, it will be increasingly difficult to find effective software. If such software can be developed, an inordinate amount of time will possibly be spent by teachers and librarians policing the use of the system. A second consideration is that filtering software often blocks very useful materials that the library would select for student access.

The School Library?

How does all of this translate to a school library? What should the librarian do? To the authors, decisions about allowing access to the Internet and other such electronic information should be made using the same criteria as decisions regarding other print and non-print materials. The philosophy of the district or school, the goals of the library, the values and wishes of the community should be surveyed if restricting access to the Internet is being considered. A school library is unique to itself and should function according to the values of the community it serves.

Questions to Be Considered

The following questions may help to direct the efforts of a school librarian trying to work through the filtering dilemma:

- Who are we? What constituencies does the school represent?
- Are there indicators as to the values of the community?
- Who are the outside stakeholders who need to participate in decision-making?
- How does the library communicate with the community?
- What is the role of the Internet in the school? In the library?
- What type of environment should the Internet help create for the library?
- What is enforceable and unenforceable?
- What is the best way to survey the community and the school?

Notes
1. Older, N. "Krug's Toughest Fight?" *Library Journal.* (May 1, 1997). P. 38.

Sample Policies and Forms

Following is a recommended school selection policy that will guide a committee in its consideration of censored books or materials(s).

Also included is a recommended censorship form that could be given to students or parents to complete when they object to a book in the library's collection or, possibly, in a classroom. If the parent or student reads the book and completes the form it will start the review process by the faculty–library committee.

Mt. Ararat High School, Topsham, Maine
Materials Selection Policy

1. Responsibility for Selection

The MSAD #75 Board of Directors is legally responsible for all matters relating to the operation of all MSAD #75 schools.

Each library collection is considered a segment of the total district library collection. All materials are shared; all materials are made available upon request to any school library in the district.

Selection of materials involves many people: principals, teachers, librarians and department chairmen. The responsibility for coordinating the selection of library materials and making the recommendation for purchase rests with the professionally trained library-media personnel.

Needs of the individual school based on knowledge of the curriculum and of the existing collection are given first considerations.

2. Criteria for Selection

Materials for purchase are considered on the basis of: overall purpose, timeliness or permanence, importance of the subject matter, quality of the writing/production, readability and popular appeal, authoritativeness, reputation of the publisher/producer, reputation and significance of the author/artist/composer/producer, etc., and format and price.

Requests from faculty are given high priority.

3. Procedures for Selection

In selecting materials for purchase, the librarian evaluates the existing collection and consults reputable, unbiased, professionally prepared selection aids as well as specialists from all departments and/or all grade levels. In specific areas the librarian follows these procedures:

1. Gift materials are judged by basic selection standards and are accepted or rejected by these standards.

2. Multiple copies of items much in demand are purchased as needed.

3. Worn or missing standard items are replaced periodically.

4. Out-of-date materials or those no longer useful are withdrawn from the collection.

4. Objectives for Selection

The MSAD #75 Board of Directors recognizes that it is the primary objective of the library media centers in our schools to implement, enrich, and support the educational programs of the schools. It is the duty of the library media centers to provide a wide range of materials on all levels of difficulty, with diversity of appeal and the presentation of different points of view.

To this end, the Board of Education reaffirms the Bill of Rights for School Library Media Programs and asserts that the responsibility of the School Library Media Center is:

1. To provide materials that will enrich and support the curriculum, taking into consideration the varied interests, abilities, and maturity levels of the students served.

2. To provide materials that will stimulate growth in factual knowledge, literary appreciation, aesthetic values, and ethical standards.

3. To provide a background of information which will enable students to make intelligent judgments in their daily life.

4. To provide materials on opposing sides of controversial issues so that young citizens may develop under guidance the practice of critical analysis of all media. (Opinions expressed in library materials are not necessarily endorsed by the MSAD #75 Board of Education.)

5. To provide materials representative of the many religious, ethnic, and cultural groups and their contribution to our American heritage.

6. To place principle above personal opinion and reason above prejudice in selection of materials of the highest quality in order to assure a comprehensive collection appropriate for the uses of the library media center.

In addition, the Board of Education recognizes that the final decision as to what materials an individual student will be exposed to rests with that student's parents or guardians. However, at no time will the wishes of one child's parents to restrict his/her reading or viewing of a particular item infringe on other parent's rights to permit their child to read or view the same material.

5. Challenged Materials

Despite the care taken to select materials for student and teacher use and the qualifications of the persons who select the materials, it is recognized that occasional objections may be raised by community members, students, or school staff. In the event a complaint is made the following procedures will apply:

1. The complaint shall be heard first by the librarian.

2. If the matter is not resolved the complainant will be given a "Request for Review of Library Materials" form to fill out. The form will be forwarded to the principal and the superintendent of schools.

3. The principal shall appoint a committee composed of the following people to review the complaint: one administrator at the appropriate grade level; one librarian/media specialist; one classroom teacher; the department head in the subject area of the challenged materials; one community member.

4. The review committee shall: read and examine the materials referred to them; check general acceptance of the materials by reading reviews; weigh values and faults against each other and form opinions based on the material as a whole and not on passages or portions pulled out of context; meet to discuss the material.

5. The decision of the reviewing committee shall be forwarded in writing to the complainant and the superintendent.

6. If the complainant is not satisfied by the decision of the reviewing committee and desires to carry the request further, the form may then be submitted to the Board of Directors of MSAD#75.

7. No materials shall be removed from use until the committee has made a final decision.

8. Cooperation will be any parent wishing to restrict his or her own child from using materials which are objectionable to the parent. The librarian, with the parent, will try to work out a solution that will keep that family's child or children from checking out the materials the parent objects to, while still allowing free access for other children.

Request for Re-Evaluation of Material

Title _____

Author _____

Publisher

Type of work

Your Name

Who do you represent?

Did you read or view the entire work?

What do you object to? (cite specific incidents, pages, etc.)

Does it have any redeeming qualities? _____ Please explain your answer: who should have access to this material, what is its theme?

What do you feel should be done with this material?

_____ return it to the committee for re-evaluation

_____ Other. Explain   _____

Chapter Nine

Gifts to the Library, Boon or Bust?

Sri Lanka – wood

Scenario 1. A prominent educator in the community has died and his family wishes to donate a collection of several hundred books and periodicals on education to your library. The family would also like a statement of value from the library to use for tax purposes.

Scenario 2. A religious denomination is willing to spend several hundred dollars for an encyclopedic work on their religion if it will be housed permanently in the high school library. The high school is public, not parochial.

Scenario 3. A valued collection of Western Americana has been offered to your library under the following conditions:

- *The collection must stay intact.*
- *It must be housed separately from the rest of the library's collections, preferably in its own room with security shelving.*
- *A donor bookplate must be placed in each book.*

Many librarians have experienced, with modifications, such scenarios, and others. Lacking policies and guidelines, librarians make a decision about each donation separately, with little or no consistency. Worse, librarians accept gifts of books and other materials which are of no use to the library at all, just to keep the "gift door" open for future donations. "Never look a gift book in the mouth," is often the motto of the money-strapped librarian. The librarian is then at a loss as to how to discard the materials without offending the donor.

One obvious answer is to inspect the gifts before accepting them. This may sound good, but in reality it is seldom a workable solution. Donors are not inclined to wait while the librarian decides whether or not to accept their largess. Rather, they expect, and deserve, to be thanked immediately. Each donor should receive an immediate oral acknowledgment as well as a letter of thanks. If this is not done, months and years of public relations efforts can be negated with a single instance of poor communication between the librarian and the donor.

How does a librarian effectively handle gifts to the library? The first step is to formulate a gift acceptance policy and have it approved by the library's school board and administration. The policy should be followed consistently, deviating only when an extremely valuable donation makes it worthwhile, and then only with the permission and involvement of those who approved the policy. (The Western Americana collection in scenario 3 may well be worth meeting the demands of the donor.)

Factors to Consider in Your Gift Policy

- Assessing the value for tax purposes is the sole responsibility of the donor, who must have a professional estimator evaluate the donated materials. Certainly, the library should have the names of professional estimators on hand to whom they can refer the donor. A librarian is not to evaluate a gift for tax purposes unless the gift is of minimal value. What is minimal value? The authors called Internal

Months and years of public relations efforts an be negated with a single instance of poor communication between the librarian and the donor.

Keep in mind there are no free gifts. Although the library does not pay for the donated materials, processing them can be expensive and time consuming.

Revenue Service offices in both Colorado and Idaho and have received the same unofficial estimate of gifts under $200. The librarian can only describe the gift in terms of quantity.

- Try to accept gifts with no strings attached, i.e., no specifics on how the library should house or use the gift. Get a commitment from the donor that the library may use the gifts in the way that best serves its purposes. The donor should be asked about the disposition of materials which the library cannot use. Public, school and church libraries as well as classrooms, nursing homes, and museums may accept donated materials.

The authors have found some golden questions to ask each donor as the materials are accepted. "What would you like us to do with the materials we cannot use? Return them to you, or is it acceptable if I find other locations for them?" In the majority of cases, donating patrons do not want the materials returned to them. They are trying to dispose of the materials, not get them back. The librarian is free to use or dispose of them. The donor will be involved in the final disposition of the donated materials and will be satisfied about how the matter was handled.

Suggest to the donor that materials that cannot be used in the library may be used effectively in the school's classrooms.

After all is said and done, the librarian should write a letter of thanks and reiterate the final agreement about the disposition of the gifts. Wording could be, "As we agreed on November 14th, the library will disperse any items we cannot use," or, "As we agreed on November 14th, we will forward to the Hamer Library those gift items we cannot use." A sample letter is included at the end of this chapter.

Keep a copy of the letter on file. While many librarians wish to have the donor return a signed letter stating the terms of the agreement regarding donated materials, this is not often feasible.

Situations where donated materials represent a specific interest group, business, religion, etc., can present a real dilemma to the librarian. While the materials may be invaluable as sources of information, the librarian may be hesitant to accept such gifts if they represent a single point of view when, perhaps, several other viewpoints are equally valid. For a school library, the problem can be alleviated by adherence to the school library gift policy. Such a policy will limit the library's collection to those materials that support the school's curriculum and will, at the same time, enhance the collection and services of the library. This gives broad leeway to the librarian and library–faculty committee, enabling them to thoroughly investigate the situation and make informed choices. A sample gift policy is included at the end of this chapter.

Dollars may not be available to purchase additional materials to balance the collection.

Should the materials support the curriculum and still represent a single view, then it becomes obvious that additional materials will need to be purchased, if various viewpoints are to be represented, and the gift in question is to be accepted. A clear and concise policy is vital to the entire gift acceptance process.

With a gift policy in place, the library benefits from the "boon," and both the giver and receiver are protected from the "bust." Compliments from donors who are treated promptly and graciously at the library will contribute to a positive image of the organization and will be valuable as a public relations tool. Moreover, donors will continue to offer your library gifts. The opportunity to expand the library's collection with the possibility of acquiring unique and valuable items is an experience that every librarian should have.

Gift Acceptance Policy

1. Donated materials will support the school's curriculum.
2. Processing time and expenses will be considered before accepting donated materials.
3. Estimating the value of donated materials for tax purposes is the sole responsibility of the donor, unless the value of the gift is under $200. The librarian can only describe the gift in terms of quantity.
4. The library will stipulate the housing or use of the materials.
5. The librarian has responsibility to write and keep on file a letter that reiterates the final agreement concerning the deposition of the gifts.

A Letter of Thanks for Gifts Donated to the Library

Dear Mrs. Donor:

On behalf of myself and the Elementary School Library, I wish to thank you for the books and other materials you recently donated to the school's library. We very much appreciate your generosity and desire to help us with the education of our students.

(*Scenario 1*) To reiterate our conversation of March 11th, the library will evaluate the donated materials and determine where they will best fit the needs of our students. Possibly, some of the materials may be included in the library's collection; others, we may have faculty members preview and give them the opportunity to use them as classroom materials. As we agreed, the materials that cannot be used by the library will be forwarded to the public library for possible use in their collection. Beyond that, the materials will be discarded.

(*Scenario 2*) To reiterate our conversation of March 11th, your donated Western Americana materials will be housed in a separate section of the library. Your offer to purchase glass-enclosed shelving will assure the preservation of your collection as well as creating a functional and beautiful display of these historical materials. A signed name plate will be placed in each book, informing patrons of your gift. These materials will not circulate but will be accessible to students and patrons in the library. We are excited to have this collection as part of our library. We assure you it will be well publicized and feel it will lend towards the library taking an ever increasing role in the education of our students as well as becoming a historical depository for the community.

(*Scenario 3*) Since our conversation of March 11th, the library has had the time to evaluate the books and materials you donated to our collection. We have found that few, if any, of the materials are applicable to an elementary school's curriculum. They could be of value to the high school. If you wish me to take the collection to the high school library for their consideration, I will be glad to do so. Otherwise, as agreed, I will return the collection to you.

I am not able to give an estimate of the value of your donation for tax purposes. It is against the law. However, enclosed are the name and address of persons who can estimate the value of the collection. This estimation can be forwarded to the IRS. Enclosed is a listing of the materials you donated.

Thank you once again for thinking of us. Do not hesitate to contact me if I can be of further service.

Sincerely,

Chapter Ten

Seeking Funds

It Can Be Fun & Effective

Mexico – wood

Very few people enjoy trying to raise money. Expectations are seldom realized and the process is not only a lot of work but it makes many people uncomfortable. However, this is not true of fundraising activities for a library. When done properly, library fund-raising can be extremely effective, and the librarian can become a willing rather than a reluctant participant. Successful fundraising activities can make the difference between mediocre and excellent library collections and services. In this era of tight library budgets, fund-raising by the librarian is often essential if the library is to achieve its role as a prime factor in the education of students. Fundraising benefits not only the school's students, faculty, administration, and community, it can also reflect in a most positive manner upon the librarian.

So what is the best way to raise funds for the library? First, the librarian must target specific needs. Never ask potential donors how much they would like to donate. Rather, select a specific item that is needed and would be of great benefit to the students and staff of the school. It should be something that would not otherwise be obtainable through the regular library budget. Research the exact cost of the requested item, be it an automated system, display cabinet, a new service, etc. Having determined what is needed and its cost, it is then possible to approach businesses, industries, or private individuals, seeking their donation for that single item. To supplement the request, have a very attractive poster to show how their donation will be acknowledged. This poster can be placed in the window of the business, acknowledging their participation in helping to educate children. Furnish a brief article and photograph to the local newspaper and ask for their assistance in reporting the donation. (However, some donors will request to remain anonymous). Often, radio and television stations will use this as a news event. The donor receives positive publicity, and sometimes a tax write-off for the amount or item they donated. As this information and publicity becomes known, you will discover that others will want to participate in the program. Asking a potential donor to help the library in its role to enhance the education of students is a simple thing to do. The appeal is obvious and the librarian may be surprised to find that the vast majority of requests will be approved.

The success rate of this program is high, especially if the librarian has tailored funding requests to the financial capability of the donors. Everyone benefits, especially the students of the school, who are the library's chief concern. A sense of community will be fostered when individuals and businesses take the extra step to help educate children.

There are direct benefits to the librarian as well. She is seen as a contributor to the education of children, a concerned professional educator, and certainly a valuable resource person to the school and community. It is one of the most effective things a librarian can do to fulfill the library's role. The library can take its place as a foremost entity in a child's education, and it may become the last place to have funding and services curtailed.

It can even be fun!

One of the greatest partners in fund raising is the local parent/teacher organization. Every librarian should make it a point to become personally acquainted with PTO/PTA board members for funding and other purposes.

Many schools have established partnerships with local businesses. Be sure the library is involved.

Writing for Grants

No section on fund-raising is complete without mentioning one of the most effective methods of achieving new and exciting library programs and services — that of grant writing. The most obvious benefit in writing grants is that the successful ones give the librarian the resources she needs to make dreams a reality. In the process, many students benefit from funded programs; librarians gain a sense of real accomplishment; funded programs offer new experiences and growth to the students, staff and librarian involved; and successful grant writing increases the librarian's professional image in the field.

The age-old library adage that "you only have one chance to make a good first impression" is especially true in writing grants. Funding foundations, corporations, and businesses can usually tell with a single review whether or not a proposal meets the guidelines of what they are trying to accomplish and thus, whether or not the proposal will be considered for funding. The reviewer's first impression of the proposal is vital to its success. Though grant writing is a skill that is enhanced with experience and commitment, good planning on the part of the librarian can make even a first effort successful.

It has been the authors' experience that library proposals which have an impact upon student achievement are those most likely to be funded. A great many funding agencies are interested in using their assets to improve education (and libraries). They are concerned with student outcomes. Library proposals that will lead to improved reading scores, research skills, teacher-librarian curriculums, etc., are prime candidates for success. When you can identify a problem and submit a strategy for solving it, then the proposal becomes a means to an end rather than simply asking for money. There is a big difference.

Another very effective "grant winner" is the proposal intended to increase local support. When you represent a single school or district, begin by seeking funding through local communities, and neighborhood businesses. Cooperative efforts between local constituencies to improve library programs and services can also be very effective. A sense of community pride and purpose can ensue which is invaluable to the school and library. For a librarian to identify a critical area of need and then find local funding to correct or institute new or better programs, gives the entire community a sense of unity and purpose. It is also true that funding entities want to see evidence of local support. Therefore, starting with community fundraising efforts will help to secure funding for larger and more complex projects in the future. Seeking local support first is one of the most effective considerations for current and future library proposals.

Research Process

Once the decision has been made to pursue foundation or corporate funding, the librarian is then ready to begin the research process. Taking the time to assure that your proposal will be sent to the entities that make grants to your type of organization, fields of interests, in the geographic area in which your library is located, will save countless hours of writing and submitting proposals. Studies indicate that foundations and corporations reject many of the proposals they receive because the proposals do not fit the guidelines of the fund-granting entity.1 Librarians must be clear about their goals, the needs to be met by their proposal, the amount of money necessary to achieve their objectives, and the availability of funds from other sources. Foundation or corporate funding does not address all projects and a great deal of time, frustration and disappointment will be saved if efforts are honestly assessed in advance.

Find out all you can about a potential funding source before you submit a proposal. Does the organization fund only in specific geographic areas? Does it grant

---

Always take a positive approach when contacting funding sources. List the strengths of your proposal, community, clientele, etc., rather than dwelling on problems and negatives.

Think small sometimes. Finding little-known funding sources will increase your chances of success.

Ask an experienced grant writer to read your proposal before submitting it.

funds in the approximate amounts that you are requesting in your proposal? Does it fund the type of projects that your proposal addresses? An effective way to find this information is to call or write a letter asking for a copy of a funding institution's guidelines or procedures for submitting proposals. Often a copy of the annual report will list successful proposals of the past year and the amounts funded. The importance of taking the time and effort to find this information is obvious. It is essential that your proposal be sent to the funding organizations that are interested in the type of project(s) for which you are seeking support.

Finding Funding Sources

Often the district office or a school principal's office will receive announcements from funding entities calling for proposals. Such announcements will state the type of projects they are funding and the amounts available. Usually, these notifications pertain to specific geographic areas — local businesses and corporations that wish to improve education with the funding they have available. Under these circumstances, a well-developed proposal has an excellent chance of succeeding.

If unsuccessful, try again and again to different funding sources.

The second approach is to actively seek funding sources for your particular proposal. In the field of grant writing, there are numerous resources available, in all types of subject areas. Perhaps the most inclusive and finest single funding resource is the following:

The Foundation Center
79 Fifth Avenue
New York, NY 10003
(212) 620-4230
fdncenter.org/grantmaker/nng.html

The Foundation Center in New York City has member libraries all over the country for public use without charge. There are libraries in each state which carry the Center's directories listing fund-granting entities, state by state. Librarians simply need to call the Center at the phone number listed above to find information on how much a foundation gives and to whom. For instance, *The Foundation Directory* is an annual and is published by the Center, listing funding entities by geographic areas as well as specific topics or projects they are interested in supporting. The Center also publishes subject directories such as *The National Guide to Funding for Library and Information Services*, which comes out every two years. This is an invaluable directory for school librarians as it lists entities in each state that fund library proposals. The directory lists donors, the type of foundation (private, independent, etc.), financial data, purpose and activities, fields of interest, types of support, limitations, and application information.

Using the Center's publications, plus keeping informed of local funding entities will enable any school librarian to find grant writing opportunities.

Notes
The Foundation Center. *The Foundation Directory.* New York: Foundation Center, 1998.

Chapter Eleven

Libraries & the Internet

William Rasmussen

Unknown – wood

A library is a place to find answers to questions, to find books to read for fun, or to catch up on the latest news. It could, therefore, be characterized as an information storehouse. The knowledge of the world can be found within a library's walls. That, of course, was the original intention. Today, we realize the wealth of information that exists in the world can no longer be contained within walls. We must reach beyond, to the world of information available through the wonderful medium of the Internet.

Internet History

The Internet began as a way to share information. Scientists and researchers were looking for ways to link information accessed by one computer to another. Thus, the first "NET" was born in 1969. It was called ARPANET, a military acronym for Advanced Research Projects Administration, since its funding came from the Department of Defense. It connected three computers in California with one in Utah. Soon other computers were linked to it, and eventually people in Washington, D.C. could access information from a computer in Los Angeles, California. In time, ARPANET went international with connections initially to England and Norway.

The key to sharing this information was to agree upon a language. An Internet Protocol (IP) was established that allowed these computers to share information with one another. All the computers connected to this network agreed to communicate in the same way.

By 1986 it was becoming apparent that the system needed to be changed. In that year the National Science Foundation decided to create their own network. They used the same language as their predecessor, but provided faster service.

Thus, the race was on. The quest for more information and faster response to inquires led to more advances in computer technology. Suddenly it was no longer a novelty to be "talking" to a computer anywhere in the world. Information was wanted and wanted *Now!*

This quest for faster service and more information moved the NET away from the sponsorship of the military and science communities to commercial industries. Giant corporations took over technical support of the structure. At the same time, what was once a "nonprofit" link to information now involved the commercial world of advertisements.

Freedom of Access

The information age has created a whole new area of concern for libraries. Historically, libraries have waved the banner emphasizing the importance of freedom of expression. As such, they have attempted to insure that their book collections are diverse. They have given their patrons the right to choose from a vast number of books and materials. Selection of these materials reflected the standard of appropriateness in the community. As such, some communities have been more liberal than others in the types of materials allowed. Because the Internet hooks the computer to the world, suddenly a patron has access to information that may not be appropriate according to community standards. Now libraries are faced with a dilemma. Do we continue to herald the trumpet of freedom of expression or do we find a way to limit

45

access to the Internet, dependent on community standards?

The United States Congress has gotten into this debate with passage of the *Telecommunication Act of 1996*. In it they attempted to legislate against "obscene, harassing, and wrongful utilization of telecommunication facilities." Part of their attempt was to establish a set of standards which would protect young people from inappropriate sites on the Internet. The courts have declared that the act violates the first amendment to the United States Constitution. Therefore, access to the Internet has been upheld.

However, the courts did give rise to the argument that libraries could restrict access to minors. They recognized the importance of protecting youth from inappropriate materials. This has led to the development of "filtering" services to which libraries, schools, and parents may subscribe. The idea behind a filter is to exclude sites on the Internet that would not be appropriate for young people to see without parental supervision. Various companies have developed computer software to provide this service.

While librarians must recognize that using a filter may be appropriate for limiting access to young people, adults need to have unrestrained access to the Internet. Therefore, it is imperative that a library's policy statement reflects this idea. Librarians should consider contacting the American Library Association (www.ala.org) for examples of policy statements, and for current information on this topic.

How to Access the Internet

When a user logs onto the computer, it means the computer has been told who they are. Usually a password is also required to complete the access. After selecting access to the Internet from a menu, and dial-up, an electronic page of information will appear on the monitor. What happens next? The computer's mouse is taken firmly in hand and navigation begins through the sea of electronic information.

In most cases, a click of the mouse point or typing a word or phrase will get one started. Since every computer system is unique, it is impossible to give specific instructions. It may be necessary to turn to a colleague or a student to get onto the "electronic superhighway."

Typically a person desiring to use the Internet or the World Wide Web (WWW) is looking for something. They want information. There are two basic methods for finding information. The first involves knowing the desired Internet site and its address. Therefore, in the appropriate location on the computer screen, one types in the address. For example, the user wants to visit the Library of Congress. Find the location on the screen where the address can be typed. Type in <www.loc.gov> and in a few seconds the home page of the Library of Congress appears. Now the computer is connected to a computer in Washington, D.C.

Internet addresses are logical—www, stands for the World Wide Web; loc means Library of Congress; gov is an abbreviation for government.

The second option is a subject search. The address is not known, but the subject is. Now, enter the world of the search engine. Just as an engine provides power for a car, a search engine provides power for words. Typing the word "dog" into a search engine can lead to more than 238,000 potential sites on the Internet. Wow!

There is, however, a difference in the search engines used. Names like Alta Vista, Excite, WebCrawler, HotBot, Lycos, Infoseek, and Yahoo are a few examples. Some search engines maintain lists of information in an attempt to organize the vast amount of data that exists on the net. Other search engines simply go out on the net and search for the key words.

Because of this difference it is important to realize a search should not be limited to just one search engine. Several should be tried to see what information they can find. There will probably be similarities, but the differences may provide the information you need.

Trying to sift through the information to get what is really wanted can be a formidable task. Hours can be spent looking at the description of each site to see if it is wanted. A better way is to more narrowly define the search topic.

As the search is limited, the power of the computer is harnessed with the power of words. For example, if the search consists of finding information on guide dogs for the blind, the list of sites could be scanned under the word "dogs" until "guide dogs" was found. A better way would be to more narrowly define the search. Instead of typing the word "dog" into the search engine, try the words "guide dog." *Whoa, what happened?* Now there are more than a million sites! That is because the computer searched for information on "guide" and on "dog." Instead of more narrowly focusing the search, it was expanded. The first lesson has been learned about search engines. It is necessary to think like a computer. To focus the search, the computer needs to be instructed to look for both words together. To do this, one method would be to type parentheses around the words (guide dog) in the appropriate location on the computer screen. This leads to a far more manageable list of more than fifteen hundred sites. Fortunately, in this case, the top ten sites lead to the information needed.

Each search engine also has additional techniques that can be used to help limit a search. Some search engines are set up to use Boolean logic. By using the commands, "and," "not," and "or" the search can be limited. To find out how to use the full power of the search engine use the mouse to click on the word HELP located on the search engine's home page.

In addition to search engines, list servers can help find the information. People are searching the Internet daily in an attempt to keep track of the location of useful information on the Internet. An example of one such list is maintained at Berkeley, California. By typing the following address, <sunsite.berkeley.edu/InternetIndex>, you can be connected to the Librarians' Index to the Internet. Here, links will be found to topics such as art, history, science, and even travel (for those spare moments when there are dreams about going to Tahiti).

When an Internet site is found which is particularly good, bookmark it to make it easier to visit frequently. The Internet browser software should provide a way to do this. Simply go to the selected site and then find the place on the Internet provider's home page that lets a bookmark be added. Click on the command Add a Bookmark, and this site's address is added to your list, making it possible to go to the bookmark file, click on the needed site and in a second, (or two if it is a busy day), be there.

In spite of the access dilemma posed by the Internet, it has opened to the world all types of information. The most important product of today's world is information, and libraries enable all segments of the population to access that information through the World Wide Web.

To Filter or Not to Filter

When faced with the decision of whether to use filtering software for Internet service, keep in mind the following:

1. Filters are "word" sensitive—they don't have eyes to see what the Web site really contains. Therefore, even simple words like "puppy" and "kitty" can bring up sites which could be inappropriate for children. Filtering out words associated with body parts can eliminate access to information that students may need for legitimate research.

2. According to the "Access to Electronic Information, Services, and Networks: An Interpretation of the Library Bill of Rights" published by the American Library Association, "Users should not be restricted or denied access for expressing or receiving constitutionally protected speech. Users' access should not be changed without due process, including, but not limited to, formal notice and a means of

Typing groups of words in parentheses tells the computer that these words must be searched together.

Boolean logic, named after the nineteenth-century mathematician George Boole, is a form of algebra in which all values are reduced to TRUE or FALSE. Boolean logic is especially important for computer science because it fits nicely with the binary numbering system, in which each bit has a value of 1 or 0. Another way of looking at it is each bit has a value of TRUE or FALSE.

When looking for a web site that must include both dogs and blind, type "dogs AND blind." If you want information on guide dogs but not training, type "guide dogs NOT training."

Words that are underlined or are in a different color on the computer screen could be links to other pages of information. To find out, use the mouse. Position the mouse pointer over the word, and the arrow will turn to a hand with a pointing finger. Click on the pointed finger for additional information.

A home page is like the cover of a book. It is designed to attract attention and motivate the user to want to read it.

appeal... The rights of users who are minors shall in no way be abridged." At the 1998 Midwinter Conference, the ALA affirmed "that the use of filtering software by libraries to block access to constitutionally protected speech violates the Library Bill of Rights."

3. Unrestricted access to the Internet, especially by youth, is an issue which has generated litigation and legislation at the local, state, and national level. It is likely to continue, and ultimately the school media specialist must reach a decision based on community and district standards. However, adopt a policy which will meet the needs of patrons, while protecting the rights of the innocent bystander.

Library Web Sites

http://www.ucalgary.ca/~dkbrown/

The Children's Literature Web Guide is an attempt to gather together and categorize the growing number of Internet resources related to books for children and young adults. Much of the information that can be found through these pages is provided by fans, schools, libraries, and commercial enterprises involved in the book world.

http://www.itcompany.com/inforetriever/index.htm

This is the most popular information resource site for librarians. It is a comprehensive Web database designed to provide a one-stop shopping center for librarians to locate Internet resources related to their profession.

http://www.capecod.net/schrockguide/index.htm

Kathy Schrock's Guide for Educators is a classified list of sites on the Internet found to be useful for enhancing curriculum and teacher professional growth. Is updated daily to keep up with the tremendous number of new Web sites.

http://www.libertynet.org/~lion/lion.html

Librarians Information Online Network. LION is sponsored by Library Services of the School District of Philadelphia as an information resource for school librarians in Philadelphia and throughout the nation.

http://www.prairienet.org/mirage/ra/html

Readers Advisory Links. The Mid-Illinois Readers' Advisory Group is a group of librarians who are interested in developing their readers' advisory skills and in promoting literature and reading for pleasure.

http://www.nicem.com

National Information Center for Educational Media

http://www.nueva.pvt.k12.ca.us/~debbie/library/research/research.html

This is a guide to doing research. Nueva's goal: To develop independent, self-motivated, disciplined learners who can recognize problems, formulate hypotheses, ask important questions, locate, analyze and evaluate information and reach valid conclusions and creative synthesis.

http://nick.sfpl.lib.ca.us/gencoll/gencoIhp.htm

Sites listed by Dewey classifications

Access the Internet: Tips and Strategies Worksheet

The Internet is a global network of computers that allows many millions of computer users to share and exchange information. Hundreds of thousands of computers linked to the Internet hold vast quantities of data that can be accessed when the search is begun.

There are two tricks to using the Internet effectively: 1)use the tools which locate available resources and 2) map out a search strategy. There are many different tools to be used—directories, search engines, or meta-search engines. A web directory is a collection of Internet sites grouped into categories. Using a directory is analogous to using the Yellow Pages or a library catalog. A directory is often the best place to begin an Internet search because it looks at a narrowed range of information. Search engines are based on keyword searches of databases that contain millions of documents and words, providing quick access to massive amounts of information. The search engines Yahoo!, Lycos, Altavista, Excite, Infoseek, Hotbot, Looksmart and Webcrawler perform more effectively when you use a structured search strategy. Meta-search engines are an outgrowth of search engines. Each search engine accesses a portion of the Internet; while there may be overlap, no two search engines will return the same results to a query. A meta-search engine accesses several engines, thereby giving the broadest return to a single query.

Search Strategies

There are three steps involved in effectively accessing information. Write out on a sheet of paper:

1. **The search topic**
   First Step: Define the search. What is the topic?

2. **The directory and/or search engines to use**
   Second Step: Decide how to access the Web. Will a web directory give the best results or is a search engine going to be more efficient?

3. **The sites and addresses where the best information is found. Evaluate as to "where, who, why and when."**
   Third Step: Create the actual search query. A simple query uses one word, while a more precise query would link several words. For a query that links several words, most directories and engines use Boolean logic. Boolean logic utilizes four primary operators: AND, OR, NOT and NEAR. Using the word AND narrows the results, while using the word OR broadens the proximity operator which finds words within a certain number of characters. Also, there are secondary operators: "double quotes" around words that are part of a phrase; a + in front of words that must appear ; a - in front of words that must not appear. Different search engines incorporate Boolean logic in different ways. Read the instruction for each directory, search engines and meta-engines for more help.

About the Author: William Rasmussen earned money to purchase the first two computers for his small high school by bringing a circus to town in 1982. Since then he has extended his knowledge of computers while working as a school counselor and technical preparation coordinator. Currently he is a junior high school media specialist, training teachers, staff, and students in the use of new technology.

Chapter Twelve

Library Security

Indonesia – wood

Certainly, a most important factor contributing to school library security is the overall philosophy of the librarian and administration concerning access to library materials. Numerous school librarians feel that an electronic security system (gate and magnetic tapes), would eliminate theft in their library. Some librarians spend a lot of time and effort to save money from the budget or raise extra funding for a security system. In reality this should be the last step in a library security plan. Such systems can be easily compromised by anyone seriously wanting to steal library materials. In the majority of cases the person involved need not challenge the security gate at all. There are far more serious security problems. Many are within the power of the librarian to remedy. Some of these include weak points in the library building, (such as a loose window screen in the boy's restroom), policies of the library, or restricted library hours. These are but a few of the problems that need to be addressed in a comprehensive library security program, none of which are affected by an electronic security system.

Policies that Contribute to Theft Problems

The following policies and procedures are contributing factors to theft in a library. Much of this was gleaned from an excellent article by Richard Boss concerning library theft.[1]

- *Restricted hours.* Budgetary restraints often make this a problem area. Libraries open only during regular school hours often have high theft rates. Libraries that are open for student use before school, during the lunch periods, and after school, help cut down on theft. If the school library is also open to the community, then extended evening and weekend hours should be made available.

- *Lock or not.* After hours, is the library door locked or is it accessible to faculty members with keys? Policies determining faculty and staff access to library materials after hours and on weekends must be considered. One librarian may be totally comfortable with circulating library materials at any time as long as she knows where they are. Another may be totally chagrined with such a policy.

- *Physical facilities.* A loose or torn screen on a restroom window allows students to throw library materials to a friend on the ground below. It would be fortunate if these materials were ever returned to the collection. The same problem exists for non-alarm exit doors, or employee entrances. Attention should be given to every window, exit, or entrance.

No matter what the setting, the determining factor is the attitude of the librarian.

Open Areas Add to Challenges

Today many libraries are located in the middle of the school in a courtyard setting, where classrooms open onto it and there are no walls or doors separating it from the rest of the building. In such an open area, library security can be a real challenge.

- *Photocopying machines.* These are perhaps the greatest single contributor to library security. If a library has machines easily accessible to students and staff, there are fewer reasons to steal library materials. These machines need to be efficient, easy, and inexpensive to operate. Students and staff can hardly function in a library with limited photocopy services. These machines contribute not only to the convenience of library patrons but also help lower theft.

- *Circulation systems.* Materials which cannot be checked out at all, and those circulated with limited check-out periods, are subject to theft. Open-stack materials, not available for check out, are also prime targets. Libraries are well advised to have liberal renewal periods whenever possible. Libraries which issue cards to check out materials must be careful and insistent they be checked in or returned once the patrons or students have moved. However, some librarians are comfortable with former students and staff continuing to check out library materials as long as they are aware of their location. Each situation needs to be evaluated.

- *Written guidelines.* Another weakness of a library security system is the lack of written procedures when there is an incident of library theft or misuse. Without written procedures, employees must exercise their own judgment because they have no basis on which to make decisions. This results in inconsistencies and, at worst, no policies for library theft, and what to do when incidents are discovered. Often, nothing is said and the situation may continue to worsen because staff are reluctant to act without guidelines. Without written procedures, there is no security program. This needs to have administrative input or approval and be school-wide in approach.

  Librarians should have specific, written guidelines to follow when dealing with theft.

- *Cameras and gates.* Many libraries have made effective use of dummy television cameras with a red flashing light. These cameras can be made to pivot and take in the entire circulation area. The electronic exit gate and camera serve to keep people honest.

A study found that prime theft and mutilation times are shortly before closing hours.[2] During these times librarians should be very observant and consistently enforce library theft procedures. Also, very good students are often guilty of library theft and mutilation. Academic grades are seen to be more important than library materials. The damage a student can do with a short length of string in their mouth can be awesome. (Students simply withdraw the wet string and place it at the left margin of any page in a book or periodical. Within five seconds the string will soak through the page and the page can be withdrawn noiselessly).

While electronic security systems do appear to reduce losses in a library, they cannot effectively reduce theft without the librarian auditing policies and procedures to discover all of the factors contributing to poor library security. Good school library security depends on the students, and students will respond in accordance with the library's policies and tolerance regarding theft and mutilation.

Notes

1. Boss, R. W. "The Library Security Myth." *Library Journal.* 15, (1980). p. 638.

2. Hendrick, C. and Murfin, M. "Project Library Ripoff: A Study of Periodical Mutilation in a University Library." *College and Research Libraries.* 35, (1974). p. 401.

Library Security Guidelines

Theft of Library Materials

1. Exit Gate Procedures

A. If the exit gate locks and rings as a patron tries to exit the library.

1. Circulation personnel will courteously ask the patron to return to the circulation desk where their library materials will be reexamined and rechecked out (demagnetized).
2. Repeated incidents will be reported to the librarian.

B. If a patron runs through the ringing and locked exit gate.

1. Try to identify the individual involved.
2. Report the incident to the librarian.
3. If the individual is identified, they will meet with the librarian and principal to resolve the problem.

2. Patrons Claiming to Have Returned Missing Library Materials

A. Interview with the librarian.

1. Patron asked to recheck for missing materials.
   Library holdings are rechecked also. Three month waiting period before reordering but the student is ultimately responsible for replacing the item.

2. Second incident. The amount of money necessary to replace missing materials is charged to the patron. Processing fee optional.

3. Patron Apprehended Stealing Library Materials or Items Belonging to Other Patrons.

A. Immediate conference with librarian and principal with possible referral to police. Parents contacted.

1. Restitution.
2. Suspension optional.

```
┌─────────────────────────────────────────────────────────┐
│                  SCHOOL DISTRICT No. 25                   │
│                      Bannock County                       │
│                     Pocatello, Idaho                      │
└─────────────────────────────────────────────────────────┘
```

DAMAGE/SECURITY REPORT FORM

INSTRUCTIONS:Please use this form to report all incidents of window breakage, theft, building damage, break-ins, suspected vandalism, and automobile vandalism.

_____   _____   _____
Building   Date   Estimated/Actual Time of Damage

1. Who was notified? (Check)

    ❏ Police   Case No. _____   ❏ Maintenance Department

    ❏ Principal (if not submitting a report) ❏ Insurance Carrier ❏ Business Services Coordinator

2. Were there signs of forced entry?   ❏ Yes   ❏ No

3. Was there any personal injury?   ❏ Yes   ❏ No

    List name and address if there is personal injury. _____

4. Description of the incident. _____

_____

_____

_____

_____

_____

5. Estimated dollar amount of damage. $_____

6. List damaged equipment if any. (Use additional sheet(s) if necessary.)

Item	Brand	Model	Serial No.	Office Use Only
1.				
2.				
3.				

7. List equipment stolen if any. (Use additional sheet(s) if necessary.)

Item	Brand	Model	Serial No.	Office Use Only
1.				
2.				
3.				

8. Who discovered the damage? _____

_____
Signature of Person Filing Report

DISTRIBUTION OF COPIES:
    White - Building; Canary - Police Department; Pink - Business Services Coordinator; Gold - Maintenance

Chapter Thirteen

Africa – wood

School Library Budgets

It takes money to create a library, and it takes money to keep it a viable force in students' lives. "Of all expenditures that influence a school's effectiveness—including those for facilities, teachers, guidance services and others—the level of expenditures for library media services (i.e., personnel, books and materials, technology, and facilities) has the highest correlation with student achievement."[1]

Without a predictable and dependable annual budget for the renewal of the library collection and services, a school library will quickly degenerate into a dismal, disorganized mass of out-dated books, periodicals, and automated systems which are of little or no educational value. Moreover, the initial capital investment in the library, often amounting to a very large sum, will have been irresponsibly spent.

Managing a school library effectively involves managing substantial amounts of money. Unless the librarian can demonstrate reasonable sophistication in the management of a library budget, she will suffer an almost irretrievable loss of credibility with those who allocate school funding.

The preparation of the budget is an annual task, but budget planning is a continuous process. Before a budget can be prepared, the librarian must make a detailed analysis of the collection and services being offered and the amount of money needed to maintain and improve them. This is not possible without collecting data which will enable the librarian to plan for the future as well as improve upon the current collection and services. Thankfully, automated library systems enable many librarians to collect necessary data for budgeting purposes. If the data cannot be gathered via automated systems, then it must be done manually.

> If a budget is to be credible, it must be defensible; the librarian must have specific reasons and justifications for each requested item in the budget.

Budgeting Systems in Current Use

So, what are the various methods of library budgeting? How can the budget be used for the optimum benefit of the schools' students and faculty? First, it should be realized that a great deal of planning is necessary before an effective budget can be requested and spent wisely. Working to accomplish budgetary goals and objectives will enable the library to remain a viable force in the education of students.

> It is imperative that the librarian consider both current and future needs when she develops her specific budgetary goals and objectives.

There are many types of budgets, but the four most common are:

The Lump Sum Budget. This is one in which the categories are very broad and the amount is not broken down into specific expenditure items. Although it was once widely used, this system provides little, if any, accountability and is used today when costs are not clearly known. It is simply the principal informing the librarian that she has a specific amount of money to operate the library for the current school year. This, of course, represents peripheral interest in the library's programs and, in effect, removes the library from serious consideration as a force in education. The salvation of the lump sum budget is a concerned and skilled librarian who will turn the lump sum into a more effective budgeting process.

The Line Item Budget. This budget is a detailed listing of every item to be purchased along with its justification and its cost. It is somewhat comparable to one's personal checking account. Though it is an item budget, it permits no flexibility and controls only those direct expenses necessary for the operation of the

54

library. Where a library operates with either a lump sum or line item budget, there is no possibility for accountability and no opportunity for finding out whether or not a library's collection and services have achieved stated objectives.

The Object of Expenditure Budget. This budget has been used extensively by many librarians. It is popular because it is easy to prepare and understand. It is based on the premise that certain resources are needed to achieve certain functions. The librarian responsible for this budget will justify expenditures by including a written statement. This statement briefly describes the way items to be ordered will help to achieve library objectives. The previous year's financial statements are used to project the new budget. The assumption of this type of library budgeting is that certain resources will always produce certain results. Sometimes, this is not the case.

The Planning, Programming, Budgeting, Evaluating System. This budget is commonly known as the PPBS budget. This type of library budgeting makes library work effective and exciting as the results are measured by emphasizing human changes rather than the cost of materials. It is a budget wherein a given amount of the total is spent in terms of satisfying student and faculty needs. Thus, the librarian is spending a generous percentage of the library budget to support materials and services based on the performance of pupils and faculty. Library expenditures are measured by how well the students and faculty attain stated objectives.

Examples

If over the years, lower and average readers in the 4th grade begin to achieve an overall gain in reading proficiency, then the money spent by the library for books intended specifically for beginning readers in the 1st through 3rd grades, would have been well spent. If an after-school faculty workshop teaching faculty to create computer-generated presentations was attended by 80 percent of the faculty, with one hundred percent proficiency, then workshop funding by the library was successful. (If indeed, the attendance and proficiency were the stated objectives of the library workshop). The results of this type of budgeting is the payday for librarians who have had less than effective budgeting experiences in their careers.

School librarians who are dealing with lump sum and other types of library budgets are challenged to use at least a portion of their budget in a given year for the PPBS. Select a faculty member with an effective (or ineffective) instructional program and support that program with library materials and expertise to the point of stated student achievements. After having witnessed successful behavioral changes by students in such programs, other faculty members will be quick to suggest and enlist library support for student achievement in their content areas. The school will see the effectiveness of the library budgetary program and the librarian will very possibly use more and more of a library budget for PPBS purposes. When combined with capital outlay, collection, and service expenditures for the future, the PPBS is a very effective budgetary process.

Notes:

1. Colorado Department of Education. *The Impact of School Library Media Centers on Academic Achievement.* Denver: The Department, 1993; and Krashen, S. *The Power of Reading: Insights from the Research.* Littleton, Colorado: Libraries Unlimited, 1993.

Chapter Fourteen

The District Library Media Coordinator

Larry Goold

Mexico – metal

The district library media coordinator has two basic responsibilities. First, there is usually a district media center with teacher services and materials collection to manage. Second, the coordinator should serve and assist librarians at the individual buildings in the district.

What the district library/media coordinator does will be determined in large part by the qualifications of the individual who is at the building level. If there is a certified librarian at each building in the district, then the job of the district coordinator becomes one of helping to mold an effective building-level library media program. If on the other hand the people at the building level are non-certified or paraprofessional, then the role of the district coordinator is that of continual training, in what David Loertscher refers to as "warehousing duties."[1] This involves the technical aspects of running the library. Tasks might include how to shelve books, how to check them in and out, how to use an automated circulation system, or how to process a new book, etc.

The district media coordinator should serve as a liaison between school librarians and district administrators.

Managing the District Media Center

The services at the district media center are managed by the district's media coordinator. The organization of the individual district will determine what services are offered. They can be many, or they can be few. Some of them could be centralized purchasing and processing of books; printing and duplication services; purchasing, organizing, and circulation of a district media collection; budgeting; circulation of audiovisual equipment; and video production. The list can go on and on. Services from the district media center are dependent on the amount of available money that is provided by the district's administration, and how the administration determines to utilize the district media center.

The successful district media coordinator must have a certain degree of political acuity.

Assisting Building Level Librarians

A district library/media program is based on the assumption that two heads are better than one. In a school there may be multiple English teachers, math teachers, or second grade teachers, but most of the time there is only one librarian. This can be a very isolating situation. The librarian will have no one with whom she can interact. A district library/media program with a district media coordinator helps to solve this problem by providing that needed interaction and support. When the building-level librarian has a problem or question, the district person is available to assist her. The district coordinator at least understands many aspects of a problem that no other teacher or even the principal will comprehend. Most of the time it's just a matter of getting a second opinion or a different perspective. Sometimes the district person has dealt with a similar situation and she can simply share what was learned from that experience.

Generally when there is a district program there will be several other librarians in the district. The function of the district program is to also bring individual librarians together to share ideas and resources, to figure out solutions to common problems, and in the process, energize each other.

Service to the District's Personnel

The concept of service is central to the philosophy guiding the district coordinator's efforts. The position is one of "delivering services and helping people."[2] This includes all other district staff members from building level librarians to teachers and administrators. The one thing they all have in common is a lack of time and a need to make wise expenditures. For instance, a district can save thousands of dollars by purchasing audiovisual equipment on bid. The district media coordinator is integral to this process by having information on recommended equipment to purchase and how to obtain the best prices. Because the district coordinator is familiar with equipment, prices and vendors, if someone in the district has an equipment purchasing question the coordinator can answer it in minutes. Otherwise the person may have to spend hours researching the question.

Another example is expertise in the operation of sound systems, etc. Because most teachers do not use sound systems on a daily basis, they may not know how to operate them. The school librarian as well as the district coordinator are there to help the classroom teacher learn how to use unfamiliar equipment. It must be noted that the goal is not to operate the system for the teachers, but rather train teachers how to do it for themselves. The teacher becomes an independent user of audiovisual equipment and does not become reliant on others. However, in the spirit of service, the district coordinator is there to help in an emergency, and serve as the resource person who will save time and money.

The most important function of the district coordinator is to provide service. The coordinator must be responsive to the needs of each individual staff member of the district. Unfortunately, in large districts it may not be practicable to address individual teacher needs. But there is a tremendous opportunity for the district coordinator to have impact on the educational process by helping teachers, librarians and principals. Just knowing there is someone to turn to for answers is a very empowering concept.

Coordinating the Building Level Library Program

The library program needs to be as professional as possible. The district coordinator can help the school librarian by exemplifying a professional approach to education. Professionalism is many things: being a positive rather than a negative influence in the educational setting; developing approved district-wide curricula; putting in place a board-approved materials selection policy; and encouraging membership and involvement in professional organizations. The most important thing any district coordinator can do is to ensure that everyone they work with knows they will do whatever it takes to benefit students and teachers.

The district media coordinator should serve on all curriculum adoption committees in order to participate in purchasing resource materials and media for the district collection.

One of the best ways to mold the district's library program is to provide the opportunity for individual librarians to network. The obvious justification for networking is to share ideas. In the *7 Habits of Highly Effective People*, by Stephen Covey, the author calls this type of sharing synergy.[3] That is where two plus two can equal more than four. It is where librarians come together to share resources, support each other, and where one simple idea can turn into many. One result is to simply validate existing programs and practices. Another benefit of networking is to realize that other people are experiencing similar problems and frustrations. Finding solutions to these problems is always a benefit of networking. It is the district coordinator's job to help librarians focus on the solutions rather than being overwhelmed by the problem.

One way to accomplish networking is to meet together often as a group. Blanche Woolls says that librarians will become "energized and revitalized" through this process.[4] These meetings help individual librarians realize they can call upon each other when they need help or have a question. This fosters a real feeling of sharing and reliance on each other. Let librarians share their successes or lessons learned from failures and share experiences that have worked, especially those that are resource based or cross curricular.

National and state associations are excellent sources of professional support. Much of the training that is done to help school librarians is done at these conferences. It is the professional responsibility of each librarian to participate fully in these organizations. They will greatly benefit from these conferences, as well as from the newsletters and association activities.

The district coordinator needs to help librarians develop as professionals, and help them to realize that education is a cooperative effort and not a competition.

> The district media coordinator should be involved in all decisions concerning library personnel.

Working with Public and Academic Libraries

Another professional opportunity is to work cooperatively with public and academic libraries. In one district it is the goal for every first grader to have a library card from the local public library. The school district provides the time and transportation for every first grade class to visit the local public library. The public library staff provides a brief tour of the library and allows every child to check out a book. Over a period of years every child in the community will have an opportunity to use the local public library and have their own library card. This entire project is pulled together by the district media coordinator.

Frequently public libraries find themselves helping the school libraries. When an assignment is given and the school library runs out of materials, the public library can be relied upon to provide additional resources. Teachers and school librarians can help these public libraries by alerting them to upcoming assignments and making sure the public library does in fact have additional resources. Online public access catalogs (OPACs) can make this an easier process. It is becoming easier for children in their classroom to use the computer to see what books the public library has.

The end result of a strong district library media program is that it enables the building-level librarians to be more effective in carrying out their responsibilities. Because of their personal effectiveness, the students will benefit with valuable life-long learning skills and gain a love of reading.

Notes:

1. Loertscher, David V. *Taxonomies of the School Library Media Program.* Englewood, CO: Libraries Unlimited, Inc. 1988.

2. Woolls, Blanche. *Supervision of District Level Library Media Programs.* Englewood, CO: Libraries Unlimited, Inc. 1990.

3. Covey, Stephen R. *7 Habits of Highly Effective People: Restoring the Character Ethic.* New York: Simon & Schuster, 1989.

4. Woolls, Ibid.

About the Author: Larry Goold is a native of southern California, but he earned his B.A. from Brigham Young University, and an M.A. in education from Utah State University. During the past twenty years he has taught in the public schools in Rexburg, Idaho; Basin, Wyoming; and Pocatello, Idaho. A majority of his experience has been as a District Media Specialist, working both in individual buildings and at the district level supervising building level media specialists.

Chapter Fifteen

Your Own Library Philosophy

Africa – wood

Every school library reflects the attitude of the librarian. Adults and students can quickly sense the "atmosphere" of a school library as it is set and determined by the library director. The librarian's philosophy towards service, staffing, working with students, faculty, and administrators is the key factor if the library is to fulfill an essential role in the education of the school's students. By far and away, the most important ingredient in becoming a fine school librarian is to develop a positive attitude towards the profession.

The excitement of librarianship is immediate but a real philosophy of librarianship must develop over time as one gains experience. Perhaps that is why it helps immensely for the school librarian to have had experience teaching in a classroom. If the librarian has had teaching experience combined with library certification, she can well appreciate the needs of faculty and students as they pertain to the library. Unforeseen circumstances, immediate help, understanding student concerns, flexibility in library use and collaboration with teachers, are all more understandable. Many school librarians feel the time spent teaching in the classroom and in the library help form the very basis of their library philosophy.

An essential aspect of the effective librarian is the ability to differentiate between managing a school library and operating one. The two concepts are essential, but totally different, and should always be kept separate, both mentally and physically, by the librarian. Managing a school library is the primary task and concern of the librarian—their raison d'etre.

> Every school librarian develops a personal library philosophy, be it deliberate or inadvertent.

> Teaching experience in the classroom is of tremendous value to a school librarian.

Important Aspects of Managing a Library

✍ Promoting the library's collections and services to students, faculty, administrators, and possibly the community.

✍ Motivating the above populations to use the library.

✍ Setting and accomplishing goals and objectives to direct the library so it will stay current with best practices; and planning for the future, thereby remaining a viable force in the school's educational mission.

✍ Involving students and faculty in the selection of library materials and services.

✍ Establishing a budget for collection development.

✍ Utilizing flexible scheduling to create curricula involving classroom subjects, library resources, and team teaching.

✍ Establishing and teaching a library skills curriculum.

✍ Maintaining, coordinating, and teaching the use of audiovisual materials and equipment to the faculty.

✍ Using and trouble-shooting computer technology in the school.

These and other tasks of managing a library frequently take the librarian out of the library, into the classroom and sometimes into the community. *An effective school librarian will spend a good portion of her time outside of the library, promoting its use to various constituencies.*

Operations

Operating a library entails those physical tasks which are necessary but should be done primarily by library aides and where appropriate, volunteers and students. These tasks include:

- Circulation of library books and materials.

- Re-shelving of books and materials.

- Processing new materials.

- Handling overdue notices.

- Pulling materials for classroom and teacher use.

- First and second level reference questions.

- Repairing books and materials.

In small school libraries, the line between managing and operating a library can quickly become blurred. A small, one-librarian school can make the librarian into a glorified clerk, much to the detriment of the school's educational mission, unless the librarian is very careful. The librarian needs to insist upon written job descriptions (or create them) which define the mission of the library as well as the role of the librarian within it. These mission statements need to be approved and signed by the school's administrator(s). In this way the administration is aware of the collection and services of the library, its role within the school's educational objectives, and the role of the librarian as she seeks to accomplish the mission of the library.

A district librarian can be instrumental in helping to formulate consistent, district-wide library job descriptions.

A Staff of One in the School Library

Many schools have only one librarian, and in those circumstances it is essential that a firm line be established between managing and operating the library. Operating a library can be facilitated by student assistants. and excellent volunteers. A solo librarian must make an active effort to find the operational help she needs in the library so she can focus on the vital tasks of managing the library.

A one-person library can often be a discouraging task if the librarian allows it to be. All of us find it difficult at times to "pick ourselves up" and keep going after several negative incidents in the library. The authors believe that a solo librarian will find support from students, faculty, and administrators for the most part, but it is necessary to find reinforcement from other professionals in the field. This is best done by communicating with other librarians in the district, city, region, state, and even nationally. How is this done? By personal friendships with other librarians; monthly meetings with other district librarians; and membership in regional, state, and national library organizations.

In addition to becoming a member of these organizations, it is important to take an active part in them. Attend library conferences, seminars, and workshops. In doing so, librarians find the "excitement" of the field, the big picture of school librarianship throughout America. This is of immense help in developing a positive approach to librarianship. Not only will the librarian find a great deal of support and assistance, but she will become aware of the many current innovations in the field of school librarianship that she can bring back to her school. Having someone to call

Sometimes, librarians feel that conferences and seminars are of limited value. However, the authors have found that diamonds exist next to stones, and one must go to the mine to find them. The diamonds are the programs that offer insight into the latest trends.

for technical help, along with someone to talk over common library problems, makes the task of managing a school library much easier and enjoyable, especially with solo-librarian schools.

The wisest money that can be spent by a school librarian are the dues necessary to join local, state, and national library organizations. It is essential that a librarian keep abreast of her field and there is no better way. The librarian will not feel alone in her efforts to serve the school and the work will be both rewarding and fulfilling. The bottom line is everyone in the school, especially the students, will benefit.

The Professional Librarian

For a school to have an effective library program, it is of paramount importance that the librarian is professionally qualified to work with faculty and administration.

This usually means a college degree with library certification, K–12. With this professional training, faculty and administration regard the librarian as a professional on equal footing with classroom teachers in educating children. Only then can real collaboration exist between the librarian, faculty and administration. Only then can the librarian give advice and direction concerning the library and its functions. Who benefits most from a certified school librarian? The students, and that is what school libraries are all about.

A recluse cannot direct a school library. A school librarian must always be on the front line, actively promoting the library. Though a great deal of work can be accomplished during the noon lunch break at one's desk, librarians cannot afford to lunch there. It is mandatory that the school librarian mix socially and professionally with faculty and administrators during breaks, lunch, and faculty meetings. Visibility is key for a school librarian and taking an active part in the school is essential to becoming one with the faculty. Also, it is paramount in developing a positive attitude concerning librarianship as well as establishing an excellent library. Getting out of the library and promoting it by attending PTA meetings, curriculum committee and faculty meetings, etc., is extremely important. Further, it is important to keep administrators fully informed of the library's programs, accomplishments, and needs. A principal should never be caught unaware of what is happening in the school library.

The librarian's mission is to establish an excellent collection of library materials for student and faculty use, as well as provide effective services. Also, she needs to establish a friendly and pleasant working atmosphere in the library—a place where students and faculty feel welcome and know that professional help is available, a library where staff, aides, and volunteers enjoy their work. Strangely enough, these two components seem to feed upon one another and where one is present, the other soon exists. Remember, a school library's "atmosphere" is easy to detect, and adherence to these management principles set the tone for a monumental contribution to students' education by the library.

School librarians should make every effort to gain certification. Every school needs a professional librarian to assist faculty and guide children.

Chapter Sixteen

School Librarians & Homeschoolers

Eskimo – hide and fur

As one examines the lives of men and women who were major contributors to America's values and society, it seems a disproportionate number of them obtained their education through homeschooling. In the eighteenth, nineteenth, and well into the twentieth century, many leading Americans were homeschooled.

Today, once again, homeschooling is one of the fastest growing initiatives in America's rural and urban areas. It enjoys increasing recognition as a respectable alternative to public education. Currently, estimates of the number of children being schooled in American homes range from 500,000 to 2,000,000, or two to five percent of the total school-age population. These percentages are supported by the Home School Legal Defense Association, with the suggestion that the numbers will eventually level off at approximately five percent of America's school-age children.[1] As of 1998, there is no indication that numbers are leveling off. Rather, the homeschooling movement is experiencing phenomenal growth in every state. As a rule, state homeschooling populations are doubling every three years.[2] Thus, homeschooling involves a significant segment of America's student population and is something that every district and school needs to address.

Since 1982, 32 states have changed their laws to be more accommodating to homeschooling programs.[3]

Why Homeschooling?

A question often posed is why do parents decide to teach their children at home? Though there are many factors, it is strongly supported that parents do so for religious reasons. James and Suzanne LaRue reported that 86 percent of parents surveyed responded that they homeschool for religious reasons.[3] Many parents feel that their children do not obtain moral and ethical training, much less religious values, in America's public schools.

Other reasons include:

• Children who have had problems adjusting to the public schools.

• Safety issues, overcrowding, and drugs in public schools.

• Parents who want to discipline their children as they choose.

• To have a "warm, loving" home environment for special needs children.

• To avoid negative peer pressure.

• To have more time for development of special talents and interests.

• Some parents feel that school curriculums have little relevance to life.

• Research has shown that homeschoolers score as well or better than their public school peers.[4]

Many educators feel that gifted and talented students will flourish under a regular curriculum. Such is not the case. It has been found that a significant number of public school drop-outs are among the gifted and talented.[5]

The Role of Educators

It is incumbent upon educators to comply and support the requirements of their various state legislatures concerning homeschooling. The fact that some families have chosen to pursue their children's education outside of public school systems, or in a combination of homeschooling and the public-school setting, does not lessen the responsibilities that educators have to assist in the education of all children.

62

Educators are invited to advertise and publish lists of classes and services in their districts which would help facilitate home-schooling efforts in their local areas. For example, school counseling and testing services can and should be made available to homeschoolers. Homeschooled students should be able to use physical education facilities such as the gymnasium, swimming pool, football and track fields the same as public school students at scheduled times. Why? Because home-schooling parents are taxpayers and are thereby fully entitled to the use of public school facilities to help educate their children. In some states, regular classes in elementary, junior and senior high schools are opened to homeschoolers to enrich their programs of study. Homeschooled and private school students may select those classes and activities in the public school setting to supplement or combine with their home-schooling curriculum. This dual-enrollment program, which is found in several states, is an excellent example of public and homeschool cooperation.

Studies have shown that there is no positive correlation between education performance of the student and the teacher's education. [6]

The School Library's Role

The role of the school library in homeschooling efforts is an obvious one. Within the philosophical framework of equal access for all students and individual help whenever possible, school librarians need to be supportive of American families seeking to educate their children at home. If there is a sense of hesitation or frustration when it comes to helping homeschoolers, the school librarian must take the time to reflect on the fact that the library's mission is to serve children. Homeschooled children are taxpayers' children who deserve the librarian's time and effort.

How Can the School Librarian Help?

1. The librarian must become totally familiar with her state's home-schooling laws and regulations. She needs to be the resident expert concerning the programs available to homeschoolers in her state and local community. Someone has to inform homeschooling families of their options. These include: dual enrollment, school and district facilities available to homeschoolers, extra-curricular activities for homeschoolers, high school equivalency programs, counseling and testing options, and college entrance requirements.

    Become the contact person for homeschooling families. Answer their questions, refer them to appropriate faculty members, counselors, or administrators. Become their liaison with the school. The librarian is the perfect "generalist" to make them feel welcome and answer their questions or be able to refer them to people who can. In some cases, this becomes a joint effort with school counselors but the librarian should always be involved.

2. Publicize library hours to the community with a special notation that homeschoolers are welcome. Place notices in public areas and newspapers.

3. Homeschooling families may or may not call to arrange a visit to the school library. If they arrive unannounced, make them feel welcome and invite them to browse through the library until the librarian is able to meet with them.

4. Plan to spend some time explaining the library's program and options that are available to them.

    a. At a school faculty meeting, discuss with faculty the possibility of allowing homeschoolers to join with appropriate age-level classes for library instruction and programs. Most faculty will not object to homeschoolers joining their classes at the library or for library instruction in their classrooms.

    b. Set up circulation procedures for homeschooling families. Obtain the necessary information to enable the library to allow total library access to homeschoolers.

    c. Include homeschoolers' input in the acquisition of library materials, the same as with regularly enrolled students.

d. Determine if homeschooling parents should be in attendance when their children are using the library.

e. Explain that all rules and procedures applying to regularly enrolled students apply to homeschoolers, unless there are unusual circumstances and special arrangements have been made.

5. Give homeschoolers and their families an orientation tour of the library if possible.

There are many other ways that the school librarian can assist in the education of homeschoolers. Each situation is unique and different methods may be required. Librarians are innovative and respond very well to new situations.

School libraries are a marvelous place to start in helping educate all of America's children. The day is coming when educators will monitor or certify demonstrated competencies rather than specifying how they are to be obtained and school libraries will play a strong role in that process.

Notes

1. Klipsch, P. "An Education Collection for Homeschoolers." *Library Journal.* 120, 2, (1995), p. 47.

2. Whitmire, Richard. "More Students Are Finding Out There Is No School Like Home." *Statesman* (July 29, 1996).

3. LaRue, J. and LaRue, S. "Is Anybody Home? Schooling and the Library," *Wilson Library Bulletin.* 66, 1, (1991). pp. 33-37.

4. Ray, B. *Marching to the Beat of Their Own Drum: A Profile of Home Education Research.* Paeonian Springs, VA: Home School Legal Defense Association, 1992.

5. Kirk, S.A., J.J. Gallagher, and N.J. Anastasiow. *Educating Exceptional Children.* New York: Houghton Mifflin Company, 1997.

Chapter Seventeen

Hiring Paraprofessionals & Selecting Volunteers

Indonesia – wood

One of the keys to having a successful school library is having reliable, honest, informed and skilled people in the right positions. Selecting the library's staff is probably the most important administrative duty of any librarian. Excellent library services naturally result when a skilled, enthusiastic staff of professionals, paraprofessionals, and volunteers work together in a positive atmosphere.

Selecting personnel takes time, effort, and sometimes, expense. Personal interviews with candidates are always preferable. However, prior to personal interviews, it is always worth the effort to contact previous employers and other references by phone. Phone references are far more personal and generally provide a more accurate account of a candidate's past performance. Phone interviews with previous employers give the background needed for asking questions and testing reactions in the personal interview with the candidate.

Plan on spending time and perhaps money in the selection process. It is essential that the right people be hired if the school library is to fulfill its mission.

What to Look For

Two attributes that are particularly important for library assistants are self-motivation and work attendance. Because they are often on their own if the librarian is working at more than one school, the paraprofessional needs to be self-disciplined and motivated to work without direct supervision. It is for the same reason that anyone in the position must also have a record of low absenteeism. It is very difficult to effectively run a school library and provide good service if one of the key players is chronically absent. Also, since some candidates, who might make excellent employees, do not communicate well in personal interviews, the interviewer will benefit from knowing more about their past performance and receiving additional assessments of their abilities. Librarians involved in the selection process often realize that the positive or negative "gut feelings" resulting from the interview, need to be substantiated by talking with others who are familiar with the candidate's work. Many library administrators can tell of close calls when they would not have hired excellent employees if all they had to go on was the personal interview. Another advantage of having written or telephone references is that they allow the air to be cleared with the candidate regarding any previous negative work experiences. Skilled employees may have been involved in circumstances, sometimes beyond their control, which resulted in less than favorable recommendations. It is beneficial for the candidate and the potential employer to come to an understanding concerning these situations, especially if the candidate's skills and work record are otherwise outstanding.

The Role of the Paraprofessional

Paraprofessionals are vital to the efficiency and working atmosphere of the school library. They are often the first people with whom the library patrons come in contact. Patrons form their impressions of the library's friendliness and effectiveness according to how they perceive the attitude of library workers. Paraprofessionals almost always out number the professional staff, and they form the backbone of the library. Great care must be used in their selection.

Paraprofessionals perform many essential tasks that support the library's services and programs. Today, they are being used not only for clerical duties, but also for

The greatest joy to any librarian is to hire paraprofessionals who, when assigned tasks, will do quality work and complete jobs on time.

diverse library tasks in almost all areas of school library operations. With proper training, paraprofessionals working under the supervision of a professional librarian are efficient and effective. It must be remembered that their training and responsibilities are much more comprehensive, detailed and demanding than volunteers.

Volunteers in the School Library

Volunteerism in school libraries is definitely on the upswing. Indeed, much can be accomplished when parents and other adults volunteer their time to assist in the library. Experienced school librarians will tell you that library volunteers can either be disastrous drains or incredible godsends depending upon how they are managed. Two important keys to success in managing volunteers are communication and training. After personally thanking each volunteer for their willingness to help, the librarian must spend the necessary time to thoroughly screen and interview each volunteer, being very specific as to the kinds of skills needed, the amount of supervision available and job expectations. The key criteria which must always be kept in mind as one deals with volunteers is that they should never be used as substitutes for paid staff. Do not get them involved in areas where full-time staff positions are needed.

For example, a community member who is an artist, mechanic, farmer, etc., could be asked to present or create a special library program, sharing their expertise with students, faculty, and possibly community members. These can be areas of incredible value to any school library program. But tasks such as re-shelving library materials, shelf-reading, cataloging and reference work are examples of library tasks that should be performed by skilled and paid personnel. If volunteers are employed in these capacities so that the librarian can simply survive, then one should freely acknowledge that this is the case in lieu of professionally trained librarians to work with faculty and students.

In Emanuel and Joyce Prostano's excellent book, *The School Library Media Center*, the following quotation is given:

> Some volunteers have Ph.D.'s and some have library degrees. Indeed some volunteers have better credentials and are more capable than the media professionals they assist. What is unfortunate is the fact that many intelligent, well-intentioned volunteers have rarely functioned as a power bloc in the school district to improve school library programs and secure media personnel through direct action with Boards of Education. The volunteer social clubs which gather together mothers who help out for two hours a week each in the library, have probably contributed to the poor growth patterns of elementary school libraries simply because they are available as substitutes for legitimate media personnel. The P.T.O. Mothers enlisted to "man the library" in the absence of staff are a definite liability. [1]

An Effective Volunteer Program

The authors have found that it is really quite simple to establish an effective volunteer program. Certainly, every volunteer should be welcomed and thanked for their willingness to help in the school library. Indeed, some volunteers have proven to be invaluable. To find these diamonds becomes a matter of spending the time necessary to train them in a single task. As the task is completed, the librarian can easily evaluate the job as to the amount of time it has taken and how well it was done. If performance was high, then additional jobs can be demonstrated and assigned. At times it can be difficult to ascertain attitude and performance, so the librarian must be diligent and consistent in her supervision. When the right person has been found, job descriptions can be developed by the librarian and the volunteer program can be well defined and become an integral part of the school library. If the volunteer has ques-

The professional librarian can guide the atmosphere of the library but cannot create it. Library workers create and maintain the atmosphere of a school library.

When accepting volunteer help, the librarian has committed herself to an extensive amount of time in training efforts.

tionable skills and work habits, they should be thanked for completing the assign-ment, with the possibility of future involvement in the library for certain tasks. This can all be handled in a most positive manner with an atmosphere of mutual trust and appreciation. When done properly, the librarian, students and faculty will benefit from a well-defined volunteer program.

Possible Tasks for Volunteers

Special presentations.

Simple book repair. (Taping spines, repairing torn pages, or covering paper backs)

New book processing. (Stamp, press pages, attach bar codes, spine labels and label protectors.

Circulation duties.

Manufacturing teaching aids for faculty and library presentations.

Creating bulletin boards.

Stamp discards.

Dust shelves.

Notes:

1. Prostano, E.T. and J.S. *The School Library Media Center.* Littleton, CO: Libraries Unlimited, 1982. p. 51.

Interview Form — Library Paraprofessional

Take note of: Dress, Poise, Self-Confidence

Tell us about yourself. Describe your educational background and work experience.

Why do you want to work in an elementary school for a career?

Why should you be chosen to work in this library?

What are the characteristics of an outstanding library assistant?

A parent comes to you and complains that his child is unhappy when you interact with him. What would you do? (Emphasizes listening)

What approaches and techniques do you use in assisting/teaching children?

You have a student who is repeatedly rude and disruptive. What would you do?

If you had problems with an overly demanding classroom teacher, what would you do?

You are in the middle of processing new books and a teacher rushes in needing help locating materials to be used immediately. What would you do?

What is the last book you read?

What are some of your favorite children's books?

Why do you want to leave your current position?

Do you have any questions?

What to look for: enormous patience, flexibility, experience, genuinely likes and appreciates differences in children.

SCHOOL DISTRICT NO. 25
PERFORMANCE REVIEW FORM

Employee's Name: _____

Employee's Position: _____ Paraprofessional _____

Employee's Department: _____ Elementary School Libraries _____

Employee's Supervisor: _____ Media Generalists/Principal _____

Date of Review: _____

Weight Factor	Standards of Acceptable Performance for Each Major Position Responsibility	Rating Supervisor	Rating Employee	Weight X Rating
	1. Assists students and faculty in locating library materials. Directs users to call number locations, suggests possible sources of information, etc. Pulls materials requested by students and faculty; prepares copies as necessary. Employee has a thorough knowledge of library collections. Students and faculty are treated in a professional, courteous and helpful manner.			
	2. Checks out audiovisual materials and equipment. Pulls materials for students and faculty. Delivers, sets up, and operates equipment as requested by faculty. To ensure proper operation of equipment, employee has a good working knowledge of audiovisual equipment. Processes return of borrowed materials (cleans equipment and makes minor repairs, and stores materials). Records are accurate and up to date.			
	3. Checks out printed materials for students and faculty. Processes return of borrowed materials and repairs materials as necessary. Shelves books and periodicals; straightens shelves as necessary. Follows predetermined building policy for the check out of materials, this policy is followed in an accurate and timely manner. Employee has a thorough knowledge of the physical layout of the library.			
	4. As directed by the media specialist or teacher, works with students individually or in small groups to reinforce concepts presented in lesson plans. Willingly assists student in completing specific assignments and promotes a positive attitude towards the library and its resources.			
	5. Helps catalog library materials. Accurately types spine labels. Accurately enters data in the computer. Ensures that card catalog data, and labels are accurate, up-to-date and accessible. Prepares and distributes overdue notices. Work is done in a timely manner.			
	6. Creatively designs and completes bulletin boards. Prepares materials for displays. Changes bulletin boards periodically.			
	7. May supervise student aides by monitoring work, assisting and guiding students in completion of work assignments.			
	8. Appropriately disciplines students in library in order to maintain proper library atmosphere.			
	9. Accurately and promptly types correspondence, requisitions, or purchase orders as assigned.			

Weight Factor	Standards of Acceptable Performance for Each Major Position Responsibility	Rating Supervisor	Rating Employee	Weight X Rating
	10. Responsibly supervises students in the classroom, cafeteria, on the playground, and other assigned areas. Responsible for supervision of students upon arrival and departure from school. Monitors activities to ensure safety and compliance with school rules. Assists students who are ill or injured in a responsible, caring manner.			
	11. Interacts courteously with district staff and all other contacts. Accepts and acts on suggestions and comments for improving performance.			
	12. Always punctual. If absences are required, informs supervisor early enough so that normal work flow is not interrupted. Attendance is regular and absences are not excessive and do not interfere with job function.			
	13. Employee is well groomed and has a neat and clean appearance. Dresses appropriately for job assignment.			
			Total	

Employee Response to Supervisory Rating. [This section gives the employee an opportunity to respond to the ratings received on the performance review.]

Supervisor Comments. [This section gives the supervisor additional space to comment on ratings given on the performance review.]

_____   _____   _____
Employee Signature   Supervisor Signature   Date

Chapter Eighteen

No Information Is Better Than Misinformation

Mexico – clay

Weeding the library's collection on a regular basis is an absolute necessity. A smaller, up-to-date library collection is infinitely more valuable and usable to any school than a large, dated collection of books and materials. One of the most important and constructive tasks involved in developing and maintaining an excellent library for student and faculty use is that of weeding out or discarding those materials which have lost their value to the collection. If weeding is neglected, the library will soon become a bibliographic morgue of limited value. Students and faculty will seldom use it and when they do use it, they will find it difficult to locate desired materials.

Critical Reasons for Regular Weeding

✔ Weeding aids in selection and is linked with effective acquisition policies. As it is done, librarians have a much better idea of what is and is not being checked out and used. This becomes invaluable information in the collection development process. Funding can be spent much more effectively when weeding is a continuous process in a school library. Librarians will recognize subject areas which need to be re-enforced and brought up-to-date as well as weeding out materials which are not being utilized.

✔ Weeding gives the library a reputation for reliability and currency. A negative impression of a school library is very difficult to change. First impressions are crucial and the librarian must be willing to spend the necessary time to assure an up-dated and attractive collection greets students and faculty. Continued weeding will establish a reputation of a current, growing collection to complement excellent library services.

✔ Weeding best utilizes available space. There is seldom enough space available for school library collections. Weeding the collection enables the librarian to identify notorious space-takers which are seldom, if ever, checked out. Weeding frees the space for new materials and makes the remaining materials easier to access. Alphabetic space breaks on the shelves between authors' last names in Easy (Everybody) and Fiction books will help students immensely in their searches. The same is true with clear, numerical space breaks in non-fiction.

✔ Weeding helps remove the impression of a well-stocked library for those people who seldom use it. Such impressions may negate requests for additional funding. "The shelves are full, why are more books needed?" can be the initial response by administrators.

✔ Weeding locates materials which need repair, rebinding or replacing.

If we want students to respect books, we must give them books they can respect.

The Task—*Start pulling!*

School librarians are well advised to make weeding decisions every working day throughout the year. With an evaluative attitude, each book handled by the librarian can be inspected for continued use. If out-dated and worn materials are withdrawn this way, the shelf-by-shelf weeding job is much simpler. As library materials are checked out, returned, or re-shelved, a critical eye as to currency and use is an efficient way to weed a school library.

When weeding, it is easiest to work by Dewey class number rather than starting at the beginning of the collection and trying to work through to the end. Weed areas that are heavily used first then move on to lesser used subjects. When taking books from the shelf, they may be separated into three categories: books to be mended; books to be discarded; and occasionally, books to be rebound.

Catalog information for books being discarded should be eliminated immediately from the online card catalog as well as the manual catalog. Books being rebound should be checked out to the bindery and notations made on the online or card catalog.

What happens to the pulled materials?

Some books may be made available for teachers to use in their classrooms, but some books truly need to be discarded. This procedure varies from district to district. Some districts collect all books and make them available at an annual auction. Some allow books to be sent home with students. Be aware that these two practices have the potential of leaving the school district open to criticism by local taxpayers. Why should money be made available for new books when the district is giving away the ones they have? Discarded books are a volatile issue. Few people outside the profession understand the importance of weeding, including faculty and administrators. It is sometimes advisable to box books and take them to the dump. However, don't do what one librarian did. She dropped a sack of discards in a dumpster behind a local grocery store only to have them returned via the district's central office. They had been found by a citizen who had been dumpster digging and was concerned to find school books in the garbage! Incineration is another possibility.

Use of Standard Lists

Many school librarians will not weed a collection without referring to standard book selection tools such as *Best Books for Children, Children's Catalog, Elementary School Library Collection, Senior High School Library Catalog* and the *Junior High School Library Catalog*. These reference books list some of the finest materials for school library collections. Often librarians will not discard titles listed in these books unless a more recent edition is available. These tools are helpful in the weeding process, but it must be remembered that school libraries exist to support the school's curriculum and that mission must remain the most important criteria for weeding purposes.

Books to Be Discarded

In weeding the collection, the librarian is responsible to do so in accordance with the policy established by the school board. Such guidelines are necessary tools so the librarian involved will not prejudice the weeding process. On the other hand, decisions need to be made and many librarians are reluctant to discard library materials, feeling they will discard something valuable. Mistakes will be made but the process is an absolute necessity.

It is far better to weed with mistakes than to not weed at all.

Some librarians involve faculty who specialize in certain subject areas to assist with final weeding decisions. In this way a second or third opinion is available for discarding library materials. Care needs to be taken, however, when faculty members are invited to assist with weeding. Often, it can compound the reluctance to discard obsolete and unused materials. *Be careful!*

Materials to Be Discarded

The word *MUSTY* comes to mind when making decisions about what to discard and what to retain in the weeding process. The acronym stands for Misleading, Ugly, Superseded, Trivial and Your library doesn't need it.[1] In addition, the following are several classes of materials which can be considered for discard:

Textbooks

The library is not a depository for textbooks used in classroom instruction. Should a teacher wish to make extra textbooks available, then it is suggested that copies be put temporarily on reserve for student use. It is the exception, rather than the rule, to catalog and put textbooks on the shelves as part of the library's collection.

Old and worn out books

A book is not automatically to be discarded because it is old or worn. Often these books are out of print and not replaceable. They can be classics of given subject areas or cultures. Such books are sent to the bindery or mended for continued use. Studies have shown that if a book's cover is old and worn, students will seldom check it out. Many librarians have surmounted this problem by having students create new book covers for old and valuable books. It is miraculous how such books begin to circulate once again as children enjoy the new covers made by themselves and their classmates.

Encourage students on a given week to check out an "ugly" book, read it, and make a new cover illustrating the theme of the book.

Unused volumes of uniformly bound set of books

These are notorious shelf-sitters. Volumes of books, often donated to the library by well-meaning patrons, take up valuable shelf space and are seldom, if ever, checked out or used. These books might be used more effectively in a classroom.

Outdated books

Guidelines will be given at the end of this chapter for dealing with library materials when new editions or updates are not available.

Old travel and humor books   Purchase new books.

Duplicates of little used books   Get rid of them!

Books that are trivial, poorly formatted, or illustrated   These books will only take up shelf space. Get rid of them.

Books that contribute to false stereotypes of women or minorities   Get rid of them.

Exceptions to the Rules

The authors believe that there are exceptions to these categories for weeding purposes. Every library, whether it is academic, school or public, should keep local historical materials. Local libraries should accumulate the most complete collections possible on the area in which they reside. Literally, nothing representing local history should be discarded. Outdated books, periodicals, journals, scrapbooks, memorabilia, etc., should be sought after, housed and displayed. Current materials describing the socio/economic status of the community should be collected. Anything that is unique relative to the local community should become a vital part of the library's collection. Cooperative efforts between libraries are often the best way to accumulate local collections. One way or another, it needs to be done and all rules for weeding and discarding are set aside when it comes to local collections.

A second area of exception is that of periodicals and other serials. In years past, a periodical was not considered for the library's collection unless it was indexed in the ***Reader's Guide for Periodical Literature.*** Today, computers have made indexing readily available for thousands of periodicals and serials, and many publications have their own indexing either throughout the year or in the December issue. Serials and electronic media are the school library's route to keeping the library's collection current and relevant. Have as many materials available as funding will allow and keep a backlog of materials as long as possible. Space available for storage will often determine this. Microform is an inexpensive way to store many years of serials.

The third area of exception is that of reference materials. Almanacs, encyclopedias, handbooks, etc., must be kept current but the historical value of reference books is also a consideration. For example, a 1969 almanac, the year man landed on the moon would be of incredible value, with little else to take its place. The same could be said of newspapers. For many valuable resources, the only economical alternative may be microform.

A Weeding Project

In 1987, a public library published the results of a weeding project in *Library Journal*. The conclusions of the study have value for school librarians today. They were published under the heading, "What the Weeding Project Taught Us:"

- Avoid purchasing and cataloging large collections for general use.

- Concentrate on purchasing eye-catching recent edition paperbacks with illustrated jackets.

- Commercially rebound books are not worth the expense. Only in the rarest of cases (reference, out-of-print, etc.) should books be sent to the bindery.

- The security system is not a deterrent in and of itself. Material must be targeted and equipment must be effectively operating to reduce theft.

- Low circulating classics and standard core titles are not going to circulate just because librarians think they are important and necessary. They must be promoted, marketed, advertised.[2]

Conclusion

Weeding is painful because librarians love books. But the overall picture is more important. Books, in and of themselves, are not the point — their use is. Once an area is weeded, there is a great deal of satisfaction looking at shelves stocked with attractive, readable, enticing books which are easy to see and locate. In fact, the feeling is so good that impetus is provided to begin the next weeding project. On and on it goes.

Notes
1. Hayden, R. "If It Circulates, Keep It." *Library Journal.* 112, (1987) p. 10.
2. Leverett, R. *Managing School Libraries in Elementary and Secondary Schools.* Boise: Idaho State Department of Education, 1982.

Some Tips for Weeding by Class

000	Encyclopedias	New edition is needed at least every 5 years.
	Bibliographies	Seldom of use after 5 years from date of copyright.
	Books about reading	Guides, etc. Value determined by use.
100	Ethics, etc.	Value determined by use. Most unscholarly works are useless after 10 years.
200	Religion	Value determined by use. Collection should contain basic information (but not propaganda) about as many sects and religions as possible.
300	Social Sciences	See that controversial issues are well-presented from all sides.
310	Almanacs/Yearbooks	Superseded by each new volume. Historical use after 5 years.
320	Politics/Economics	Books dealing with historical aspects, determined by use. Timely or topical material: after approximately 10 years. Replace with new editions when available.
340	Government	10 years. Watch for new material to supersede older titles.
360	Social Welfare	Weeding depends on use. Most non-historical items should be discarded after 10 years.
390	Folkways	Keep basic materials; weeding depends on use.
400	Languages	Keep basic material; weeding depends on use.
500	Pure Science	Except for botany and natural history, science books are usually out-of-date within 5 years. Try to keep collection current by discarding and purchase.
600	Inventions, Medicine	Five years, unless book contains material of historical value.
621	Radio, Television, Computers	Five years at most; progressing too rapidly to be of use longer, unless in demand for historical reference.
630	Farms, Gardens, Domestic Animals	Keep up-to-date with new editions and new materials to replace older.
640	Home Economics	According to use. Keep mostly current materials. Keep most cookbooks. Consider withdrawing older books on grooming, beauty tips, fashion, textiles.
650	Business	Ten years.
660	Chemical, Food Products	Five to ten years, according to content.
700	Art, Music, Sports	Keep basic material. Dated sports material, especially about personalities who are no longer popular should be removed. Hobby and craft books date themselves.
800	Literature	Keep basic material. Withdraw older on speech making, report writing. Older volumes of Shakespeare are frequently hard to read because of small print. Update them.
900	History	Depends on use and needs of community and on accuracy of fact and fairness of interpretation.
910	Travel and Geography	Discard travel books over 10-15 years old unless useful from historical point of view or of interest as personal accounts. Update to reflect major world changes.
940-990	History	Depends on use and needs of community. Only outstanding World War II materials should be left by this time. Best materials are now incorporated in regular histories.
	Biography	Unless subject has permanent interest or importance, discard as soon as demand subsides. Replace biographies of mediocre literary value whenever better ones appear. Keep those which are outstanding in content or style as long as they are useful.
	Periodicals, Newspapers	Keep for 5 years those that are indexed. Keep others only if your patrons keep them in demand.
	Pamphlets & Vertical File	Weed roughly according to the suggestions or for non-fiction materials stated above. Keep only up-to-date material.
	Government Documents	Order and discard according to use and requests of patrons.

Chapter Nineteen

A Teacher's Perspective on School Librarianship

Mary Jo Pearson

Africa – wood

One of the goals of education is to enable students to gain the level of literacy essential to function effectively in the world and to enrich their lives. Achieving this goal requires a dynamic relationship between teachers, librarians, parents, and students. A reciprocal supportive relationship between the classroom teacher and librarian is a vital link in enabling students to achieve their literacy potential. Everyone benefits when the librarian and the classroom teacher work together to enable students to attain this goal.

Classroom teachers, parents, and librarians all play a role in developing a passion for reading in children. Motivating reluctant readers is a challenging aspect of this. The school librarian has a captive audience for dramatic book talks and lively puppet shows to introduce new books. There are many opportunities for collaboration between the classroom teacher and librarian. For example, a third grade teacher begins a "Women in History" unit in March. The students will read biographies and create a book project to present. The teacher provides guidelines, ideas, and examples of projects that facilitate individual student choices. The librarian pulls appropriate books, and gives a brief whole class book talk introduction on each one. Student interest in a particular person is sparked through the book talks and they are now motivated to read a book to learn more about the "subject" of their report. Librarians can guide student book selection according to teachers' requests throughout the school year, as long as teachers communicate current classroom themes, genres and content area topics.

Teachers and librarians collaborate and both play a role in motivation and book selection based on classroom curricula.

The school librarian is the logical teacher of reference skills and the library is the ideal setting. Materials and resources for hands-on learning activities are organized and readily available in the library. This provides an opportunity for the librarian and the classroom teacher to collaborate in designing objectives or lessons which support classroom curricula. Effective learning activities can be designed which apply reference skills to current classroom topics and curricula. For example, a sixth grade teacher is teaching a unit on Egypt. Students are creating three-dimensional projects accompanied by reports as part of the unit. The classroom teacher guides them in student-centered topic selection. They will be applying various reference skills throughout the progress of their projects. The librarian designs and guides the application of reference skills within the topic of Egypt. Reference skill objectives are coupled with content area objectives and taught and reinforced by both the classroom teacher and the librarian.

The teacher and librarian meet to design reference skill objectives appropriate to the project.

During weekly scheduled class library periods the librarian is the teacher and the library becomes the classroom. During these library class periods the librarian is responsible for classroom management and should have a plan in place. If a student requires dismissal from library class, the librarian's classroom management plan should provide for this. Students cannot be automatically sent back to the classroom as the teacher may not be there. When students are attending classes in the library, the teacher may or may not be in attendance. Often, classroom teachers utilize that time period to prepare materials, work on plans, or meet with administrators or team teachers. The librarian should inform classroom teachers of the library discipline plan at the beginning of the year. Librarians and teachers could collaborate on a plan that works for all involved. One school has a partner teacher support plan, (two classroom teachers are paired as partner teachers). When a student loses their privilege to participate in classroom activities, he/she is sent to the partner teacher's class along with their work for a specific period of time. The partner teacher support plan includes the librarian as well. The librarian can send students to the classroom teacher's partner teacher if they have lost library class privileges that day. Any plan that is effective for students, librarians, and teachers can be implemented. Librarians and teachers can work together to communicate needs and formulate a plan.

Library Acquisitions

One of the most valuable ways a school librarian can support classroom curricula is in the area of new acquisitions. The librarian can influence which books and materials are purchased for the school library in numerous ways. She can elicit wish lists from teachers and place those requests as a priority for purchase. The librarian can also suggest titles that support grade-level curricula, as she is the primary recipient of catalogues from publishers of trade books and audiovisual materials. At one elementary school, teachers and administrators place school-wide emphasis on a literature-based language arts program which utilizes trade books as the primary resource. The librarian works with each grade level committee to develop a list of trade books for study. The lists are coordinated so that there are no duplicate titles across grade levels. Each year multiple copies of a single title are purchased with library funds and housed in the school library for easy access by all teachers. This process also keeps the librarian abreast of which specific titles are studied at each grade level, and those books provide a springboard into reference skill instruction by the librarian.

> The librarian can suggest new titles for acquisition that support grade level curricula.

Another way the librarian can support classroom teachers within the scope of new acquisitions is in developing, purchasing, and housing a professional library. An effective professional library includes professional journals as well as reference books on a variety of topics such as classroom management, parental involvement, physical education games and activities, conflict resolution strategies, and up to date information and strategies on inclusion and other current issues in education. The librarian could work with the principal and a professional development committee in developing, purchasing and updating journals and books for the professional library. The school library is the ideal location to house the professional collection as it allows materials to be checked out by teachers and monitored by library staff.

New acquisitions are not possible without adequate funding. The school librarian works as an advocate for the library, underlining the importance of constantly updating resources, materials, and technology as well as promoting fundraising ideas to accomplish this. The librarian can also influence the earmarking of funds for library acquisitions by working with the local parent-teacher organization and other fund raising entities. The P.T.O. of an elementary school organized and sponsored a school-wide spellathon to raise money for media materials. The teachers promoted the idea to students and organized the spellathon in their individual classrooms. Students collected pledges for correctly spelled words. The librarian elicited teacher requests and developed a schoolwide "wish list" which included books as well as audiovisual and multimedia equipment. Several thousand dollars were raised and many of the requested items were purchased. The librarian played an important role in ensuring that teachers' requests were not only considered but given priority when it came time to allocate funds from the spellathon. Teachers, administrators, the school librarian, parents, students, and community members worked together in a successful fund-raising effort.

In addition to participating in special events such as library fund-raisers, the librarian supports the classroom teacher in numerous ways on a daily basis. As teachers request resources for particular units of study, the librarian ensures that all relevant materials are provided, coordinating reserve requests as well as satisfying short notice requirements. Whenever a student needs a book or reference on short notice he/she should be able to go to the library and check it out even if it is not the class' scheduled library time. If a district level media center exists, requests for materials as well as delivery and pick up from there will be funneled and monitored through the school library. By keeping catalogs and location procedures up to date the librarian provides a valuable service to teachers and students and supports classroom curricula.

The librarian can also schedule use of the library when library classes are not in session. A middle school science teacher invited a wildlife photographer to present to the science club. The presenter had studied and photographed grizzly bears at a reserve in Alaska. He had compiled an exciting slide show and informative commentary. The teacher reserved the library for the presentation and it proved to be the perfect setting for the educational multimedia presentation. In addition to scheduling the library for presenters, teachers can coordinate with librarians to display special classroom projects in the library. As dioramas, sculptures, or other three-dimensional projects display attractively on the tops of book shelves, they capture students' interest, aesthetically enhance the library environment, and showcase classroom learning activities.

> Librarians must be knowledgeable and able to assist faculty and students with educational media and technology.

Beyond the Walls of the Library

Accessing information, resources, and materials within the school library or district media center connects students and teachers to only an iota of the information available today. Students and teachers need access and skills to tap into the constantly expanding world of information beyond the library. The Internet provides an important link to this expanding world of knowledge. If access to the Internet cannot be made available in every classroom, the library is the logical location for Internet access. Teachers and librarians need the technology skills necessary to provide up to date information in their own lessons and also to teach these skills to students. The librarian can provide technology support to teachers and students in various ways. Many libraries have several computers which are connected to the Internet and available for student use. The librarian and the classroom teacher can work with individuals or small groups of students in the library searching the Internet for information for reports, projects, or topics of interest. Students may need help in narrowing their search for particular information and resources. The librarian can also keep abreast of relevant Web sites and post them or provide teachers with a list. Expanding the collection of curriculum-related CD-ROM programs is another way of supporting classroom curricula.

Multimedia and Literacy

In addition to providing a vital link to the information world, the library can be a center for the creative use of multimedia. Teachers and librarians can videotape students and teach them how to use video cameras and multimedia software to produce their own shows. They can also put together slide shows and presentations for use in their own instruction or when presenting to parents or colleagues. In one school, fifth grade students prepared a presentation for parents on a back-to-school night using a multimedia software program. Whenever possible the librarian can make the library available as a place to do the videotaping or presenting as well as assist in the process.

> The library is the lively hub of literacy activity as librarians and teachers support each other in helping students achieve their literacy potential.

The school library can be a lively center of literacy and the librarian is the primary person in developing it as such. It can be the meeting place for book discussion clubs, Internet clubs, or audiovisual clubs. The librarian can sponsor read-ins, book jacket design contests, diorama, or videotaped book "report" contests. The library can be the setting for cross-age tutors to read with their younger partners, or community member mentors or grandparents to read aloud to students. Literacy-related service learning projects can start in the library and reach out to the community. One school club met in the library and decided to raise funds to purchase and develop new parent "book bags" which included information on the importance of reading aloud to children and a picture book appropriate for young children. The possibilities for library-centered activities are numerous and the librarian is the inspiration and plants the seed for these types of activities. However, she does not do it alone but instead works with teachers and parents to bring the ideas to fruition. The process of helping students achieve their educational potential involves an actively interwoven relationship between librarians, teachers, parents, and students.

About the Author: Mary Jo Pearson is a reading specialist with ten years of teaching experience. She received her Master's degree in reading from Idaho State University, where she also taught courses in children's literature and content area reading. She is currently teaching third grade at Lewis and Clark Elementary School in Pocatello, Idaho.

Chapter Twenty

Library Planning

Indonesia – wood

Every school librarian should be involved continuously in the planning process. Without scheduled and consistent planning sessions, school librarians inevitably fall into the pattern of crisis management, often without realizing it. Each problem arising in the library is resolved on its own merits; and this situation often leads to a disastrous lack of consistency. Time after time, as the same problems arise, different and conflicting decisions may be made and it is not long until this lack of consistency, which is a definite sign of inadequate planning, has a detrimental effect upon the services of the library. If several hours of a librarian's working day are spent dashing about to put out large and small "fires," there is a need for more and better planning.

Planning is an exciting, difficult, rewarding, and time-consuming process. It is the basis of any school library, and it reflects on all other functions. There is a discernible, purposeful working atmosphere in school libraries where librarians have identified goals and objectives. By working to achieve specific goals within a certain period of time, librarians are fulfilling the planning responsibility.

In contrast, many librarians may emphasize current operations at the expense of planning, or they may feel there is no time to devote to planning because they are too busy with the present. Some librarians feel that planning is reserved for administrators. All of these attitudes are common in school libraries. Where such attitudes exist among school librarians, the library is relegated to a world of snap decisions and crisis management.

Robert Stueart and John Eastlick stated in their book, *Library Management*, the following: "Because of successful operations that resulted from an overabundance of funds, librarians have often been led to attribute these successful programs to their own imagination and intuition. Lack of success, however, is often blamed on 'circumstances beyond our control' instead of on the lack of planning."[1]

What Is Planning?

Planning is the process of identifying goals and objectives (Where do we want to be?), developing programs or services to achieve the objectives (How and when do we want to get there?), and evaluating the success of those programs by the objectives. (Are these programs leading us towards our goals?). Very simply, it is deciding what to do, how to do it, when to do it, and who will do it. The entire process should be written down. As part of the planning process, it is recommended that school librarians first develop a written mission statement. It could include background information, strengths, weaknesses, general purposes of the library, its raison d' etre. This mission statement is an essential step in developing a philosophy from which goals and objectives can follow.

The most common problem in library planning is the need to obtain an accurate picture of exactly what is being done. Librarians must be able to formulate their goals and objectives based upon reliable data. Therefore, there is the need to develop data gathering techniques, which must be accurate, inexpensive, and unobtrusive. They can range from a manual tabulation, to use of online circulation data and statistics. Whatever system is used, it must be monitored closely for consistency and reliability. Gathering data, sometimes a burdensome step in the planning process, has been

There are so many interruptions in a librarian's day, that without planning, patrons gain the impression that the librarian is unorganized.

Some important planning by-products are frequently noticeable, such as higher employee morale, increased productivity, and often a friendlier, more efficient atmosphere.

greatly facilitated by the use of computers and the development of in-house systems for keeping statistics. Often, a representative sampling of areas or procedures gives sufficient data for meaningful decisions. For instance, scattered weekly tabulations may suffice for library data gathering purposes, making it easier to record statistics over a long period of time.

The next step is to establish goals and objectives and to implement them. Goals are the philosophical foundations for operating a library. They provide direction, accountability, and incentive for library programs and personnel. They are not operational by themselves, but need objectives and assigned tasks in order to be achieved. Goals are long-range guidelines, often for periods of five years or more. They may or may not be fully accomplished because of changing needs and priorities. Goals are often very difficult to measure, and in some cases, cannot be measured at all. Nevertheless, establishing goals is essential for keeping a school library on track toward its ultimate purpose or mission. Make certain the established goals are consistent with those of the school, or planning efforts will be futile.

> Planning should include staff and student input.

Objectives are long or short range steps that lead toward ultimate goals. Accomplishing objectives requires that individuals be given definite responsibilities and tasks. Objectives are usually short range, specific and measurable. Thus, implementation of the planning process involves translating objectives into programs that will achieve established goals.

After implementation of the planning process, the last step is evaluation. Goals and objectives must be periodically reviewed and revised to meet changing needs. Otherwise, the library will continue programs that may no longer be effective or relevant. Some programs may need modification because of changing priorities and circumstances.

> Flexibility is the watchword. Do not get locked in with outdated goals and objectives.

What Does Planning Accomplish?

✍ Planning provides response to uncertainty and change.

✍ Planning focuses attention on library goals and objectives.

✍ Planning serves as a basis for determining the school library's accountability.

✍ Planning establishes priorities for funding.

✍ Planning facilitates a better decision-making process.

✍ Planning orients the school library toward the future.

While all school librarians sense the need for planning, the problem is motivating them to do it. If directional efforts do not come from administrators, then a grass-roots movement may be the best way to start the planning process. For example, a school librarian may establish a goal to have her collection reflect the type of community the library is in (agricultural or urban). An objective may be to acquire a strong collection of historical, social, and economic materials related to the area. Planning could include searching the available literature pertaining to the area, visiting other libraries, seeing community members, gathering reports, and histories. When goals are written into objectives and a time frame is obeyed, improved services will result. In several ways, the planning process is essential to the continuity and progress of the school library. "Tomorrow's libraries will be the result of today's planning,"[2] is a truism that must be recognized and grasped by every librarian.

Notes

1. Stueart, Robert and John Eastlick. *Library Management*. Littleton, Colorado: Libraries Unlimited. 1981.

2. Ibid., p. 37.

Example of a Long Term Goal and Objectives to Achieve It

Goal

The school library's collection and services will include materials pertaining to the local area and community which it serves. The school library will become a depository for historical as well as current community materials.

Objective #1: The library will initiate community and student support for this goal. Gathering historical and current materials will need to be both a student and community effort.

    a. A committee will be selected with an elected chairperson. The librarian will serve as secretary.

    b. Members of the community will serve on a volunteer basis.

    c. A director for student support will be appointed from the committee.

        1. District and parental permission for student involvement will be obtained.

Objective #2: Members of the committee and students will gather local histories, publications, artifacts, family histories, newspapers, and stories portraying the community's background.

    a. Materials will be stored and displayed in the "_____ Room" of the school library.

    b. All materials will be cataloged in the school library catalog. Those materials not located at the school library will be so designated and the location will be noted. (Online) District and city offices will be petitioned for adequate funding to catalog the collection.

    c. Speakers will be invited to present programs concerning historical events, no longer used skills, products, and accomplishments of the past.

Objective #3: Students and members of the committee will gather local area ethnological materials, (origins and characteristics of racial and cultural groups) both historical and current. They will also collect any geographical or geological information that is unique to the community.

Objective #4: Students and members of the committee will gather materials concerning the current status of the community.

    a. Current newspapers, books, periodicals, media, and newsletters which portray the community today.

    b. Speakers will be invited to present programs on the events and culture of the community.

Sample Mission Statement

This example of a school mission statement is provided along with a mission and vision statement of a school district. The reader will note that the two documents are in close correlation. Therefore, the mission statement of the school library is a valid one and can be used for planning purposes.

Philosophy and Mission Statement
_____ School Library

The resources and services of the library are a fundamental part of the educational process. The focus of the library program is on facilitating and improving the learning process with emphasis on the learner: on ideas and concepts rather than on isolated facts; and on inquiry rather than on rote memorization.

The availability of many materials in a variety of formats gives students and teachers the opportunity to select from among many resources the best media suited to answer specific needs. The value of each resource lies in its knowledge-building and its knowledge-extending potential. The value of the school library is the availability of the appropriate materials at the right moment for each child when he needs it. This makes the library an active force in the educative process.

The following objectives give purpose and direction to the library program:

1. To provide boys and girls with the library materials and services most appropriate and most meaningful in their growth and development as individuals.

2. To stimulate and guide pupils in all phases of their reading that they may find increasing enjoyment and satisfaction and may grow in critical judgement and appreciation.

3. To provide an opportunity through library experiences for boys and girls to develop helpful interests, to make satisfactory personal adjustments, and to acquire desirable social attitudes.

4. To provide library resources which will stimulate and promote interest in self-directed knowledge building.

5. To help children and young people to become skillful and discriminating users of libraries and of printed and audiovisual materials.

6. To provide a planned, purposeful, and educationally significant program for teaching library skills as a progressive continuum of related fundamentals from kindergarten through grade twelve.

7. To work with teachers in the selection and use of all types of library materials which contribute to the teaching program.

8. To participate with other teachers and administrators in programs for the continuing professional and cultural growth of the school staff.

9. To participate effectively in the school program as it strives to meet the needs of pupils, teachers, parents and other community members.

School District Number 25 Mission Statement

School District Number 25, in cooperation with the family and community, is dedicated to educating the whole child with special emphasis placed on dignity and self worth. We stress acceptance of differences, we emphasize cooperation with and concern for others, and we encourage a sense of commitment toward the larger community. Above all, we prize the unique worth of each individual.

We seek to provide a challenging curriculum with flexibility to meet the needs of each student. We believe that to be effective, education must be founded on secure mastery of basic academic skills, taught in integration with one another. We place strong emphasis on reading, personal expression of ideas through speaking and writing, and the mastery of computational and problem solving skills. We also encourage scientific exploration, artistic creativity, and physical activity. In every area we stress independent thinking and evaluation balanced by receptivity to the ideas of others.

Our high expectations for academic achievement are balanced with a growing awareness of others. We seek to develop in students a broad sense of the world and the obligation to perform service and function within a democratic society. We want children to realize the importance of standing up for their beliefs, as well as the value of quiet reflection.

Our District is committed to providing an atmosphere that is safe, informal and friendly, a professional staff that is constantly learning and growing, and an environment where children work together and respect one another. We strive to reach each child through recognition of and respect for different learning styles.

We believe in the worth of every individual and in nurturing well-rounded, self-respecting, caring and sensitive students.

School District Number 25 Vision Statement

Students graduating from School District Number 25 should be competent in basic academic skills, including mathematical and scientific reasoning, problem solving, reading, writing, listening and speaking. They will recognize and appreciate the uniqueness of each individual. They will care about and have a desire to serve. They will possess mental and physical skills and abilities necessary to be positive contributors to their families, communities and nation. They will have the ability to pursue learning, be prepared to lead full, productive and responsible adult lives and to feel success and happiness.

Chapter Twenty-One

Evaluation

How Well Is Your Library Doing What It Claims to Be Doing?

Africa – wood

Because of the decreasing cost of technology, school libraries are no longer isolated and distant from the greater library resources of large population centers. Through the Internet, CD-ROM programs, local, regional, and national networking opportunities, school libraries can provide state-of-the-art informational services for the students, faculty, and the community they are serving.

Discovering how to best serve this clientele and remain a dynamic source of information and service, can be summed up in one word—evaluation. How long has it been since your library has had a formal evaluation of its services and programs? If the answer to this question is not within the past five years, then it is overdue for an in-depth appraisal. Evaluation of library programs and services by the library staff should be a continual effort, as quality and quantity are never absolute, but are constantly changing. Within every five-year period, a library needs to ask its administration, its staff, and its students how well it is doing. Suggestions for improvements and future priorities must be sought.

All evaluation efforts must be based upon the overall philosophy of the library. There should be a written document that outlines the purposes of the library, and its role within the educational mission of the school. This is the "map" which gives the school library the directions to meet its goals and objectives. It is absolutely necessary that evaluation be based on stated objectives. "Without measurable objectives and without the standards of expected performance to back them up, evaluation cannot really be meaningful, or a valid part of the feedback, self-improvement, and continuous quality control."[1]

Evaluation of library programs and services requires prior planning and goal setting. Once the library's goals and objectives have been identified, then evaluative efforts become very informative, meaningful, and become a measurement of progress towards goal achievement.

Often evaluation brings to mind a grading process which makes some librarians uncomfortable. If library programs are being evaluated, the librarian who is responsible for the programs is apt to feel she is being personally judged. Therefore, the attitude of the librarian is often the most fundamental barrier to evaluation. Mae Graham, the Assistant Director of the Division of Library Extension at the Maryland State Department of Education, suggests that evaluation be thought of as a tool to measure the impact the library's services are making, and this helps to determine the library's direction.[2] This is a far more comprehensive outlook concerning evaluative efforts than attempting to grade the librarian.

Who does the evaluation? Everyone—continuously! It should never be a one-shot affair. Patron surveys or library questionnaires may be a single component during an evaluation. However, each day as the librarian instructs classes in library skills, processes materials, and conducts daily routines, evaluation should occur. As each book is handled, its state of repair can be noticed and its value to the curriculum or overall collection determined. Improvements in processing, student instruction, and faculty involvement should and can be evaluated on a day-to-day basis.

Student, faculty, and administrative feedback about library programs and services is essential if the library wishes to serve them well.

Library evaluation is a tool to measure the impact the library's collections and services are having upon the school's educational objectives. It will help to determine the library's direction.

Another barrier to evaluation is the belief that it must be comprehensive. To evaluate the entire library and all of its programs and services is to undertake too much at one time. Many times it is necessary and valuable to concentrate evaluative efforts on one program or one aspect which is a much more manageable task. Since evaluation is a continuous process, focusing on a given aspect lends towards specific goal achievement.

A third barrier can be the mistake of comparing the library's collection with its services without realizing that each has very different goals. Also, quantity should seldom be evaluated by itself. Comparing numbers of what is available now with what was available previously gives a false sense of achievement which is often not realistic. Comparing the quantity and quality of a reference collection to that of the library's general collection could be apples and oranges. A better comparison is what impact the collection or service has made upon students and faculty.[3]

The authors feel the following simple diagram to be very effective in efforts to evaluate the library's collection and services.[4]

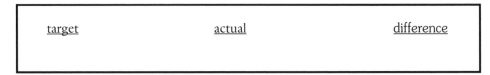

The *target* is (1) the area of the library you wish to evaluate, and (2) the standards or goals you wish to achieve. It should be measurable (i.e., expressed in a number) or at least observable. *Actual* is the result of your evaluative efforts. It is reality, or where you actually are. The *difference* is what you need to improve to bring it in line with the target data. If the difference is negative, attention must be given to areas such as planning, improvement or budget priorities. If it is positive, it becomes a measurement of what your library has achieved.[5]

A second diagram has also been found to be very useful in library evaluative efforts. It represents an attitude on the part of the library staff as well as a method of working with whatever resources are available to improve the library's services.

```
user needs        library capabilities      what can be accomplished
```

The library's resources or capabilities may be very limited in comparison to what is needed. However, there is always something that can be done with the resources that are available. The library's collection and services can always be improved. Perhaps a library with a minimal book budget can add analytic entries in its catalog for each subject area of its new books, thereby increasing the library's subject access many times over. An example would be a new book titled *Wild Animals of Idaho* which has nine chapters, each dealing with a different wild animal found in Idaho. The librarian then makes nine additional subject entries for the online or card catalog, one for each chapter or animal, and places them in the catalog referring the patron to *Wild Animals of Idaho.*

Perhaps fund-raising activities by the librarian can open new resources for the library's collection and services. Examples include book fairs, asking members or businesses of the community to adopt a periodical for student use, or inviting a business to become a partner in education with your library, to name but a few. Something can always be done with whatever resources the library has.

If the library's resources of capabilities are limited, evaluation can help determine what to do with available resources.

Evaluation of the library by its staff is all-important to ascertain the degree of success the library has made towards its goals. Planning and evaluative meetings should be held on a regular basis by the staff for obvious reasons. However, looking through the eyes of library patrons, and trying to see the library as they see and use it, is the acid test. To the authors, evaluative programs that do not have patron input are of limited value unless the evaluation is seeking an entirely different goal. Student, faculty, and administrative feedback about library programs and services is essential if the library wishes to serve them well.

How Is It Done?

Planning and evaluation are done subjectively and objectively, formally and informally. Examples of numerous survey instruments are available in published texts, and are found in district and state library offices. The authors feel that library staff can develop equally valid instruments which are often more informative as to local community needs and resources.

Perhaps the greatest benefit that comes from an evaluation study is the exchange of ideas and sharing of experiences by the library staff and its patrons. Communication is always the most important product of evaluation. To meet the needs of current students or clientele, you must meet the needs of a contemporary society. Though the purpose of any library or media program remains unaltered— that is to meet the informational needs of its users—the availability of programs and services were, in most cases, vastly different five years ago compared to what is available and cost effective for libraries today. "Technology has caused changes in every facet of library work: services, management, collection development, facilities, and personnel."[6]

The declining costs of direct access to online databases, indexing, and full-text retrieval through CD-ROM, and the Internet allows the smallest library to access vast fields of information for students and patrons. Libraries throughout America are no longer limited to any physical environment or even to local populations. One certainty is that library patrons will become more and more aware of today's informational services. If the library holds no evaluations concerning mission and programs, it will quickly lose touch with patron needs and become simply a depository. That is not what libraries are all about.

Notes

1. Taggart, D. *Management and Administration of the School Library Media Program*. Hamden, Connecticut: Library Professional Publications, 1980.

2. Graham, M. "Changing Perspectives on Program Evaluation." Speech presented to the Kansas Library Association Supervisors Section, Kansas City, Missouri, 1989.

3. Ibid.

4. Robbins-Carter, J. and Zweizig, D.L. "Are We There Yet?" *American Libraries*, 16, (1985). p. 124.

5. Ibid.

6. Eisenburg, M. *Trends and Issues in Library and Information Science*. Syracuse, NY: ERIC Clearinghouse on Information Resources, 1990.

Supplemental Materials

The following are a few sample questions for a school library evaluation, (not meant to be all inclusive).

Library Evaluation by Principals

1. How would you rate the general appearance of the library?

    Poor_____ Fair _____ Good _____ Excellent _____

2. The library should have a warm and inviting atmosphere. How would you rate the atmosphere of this library?

    Poor_____ Fair _____ Good _____ Excellent _____

3. On a scale of 1 to 10 (ten being most positive), how would you rate the librarian-pupil relationships? _____.

4. Is the library easily accessible before, during, and after school?

    Never   Sometimes   Often   Very Often

5. How would you evaluate the extent to which teachers and the librarian(s) serve students as to their interests and class assignments? (1-10) _____

6. Does the librarian inform teachers of new materials as they are acquired?

7. Does the librarian meet with faculty in curriculum planning or other meetings?

8. Does the librarian involve faculty members in the purchase of library materials?

Evaluation by Faculty

1. Evaluate your students' attitudes about going to the library.

    Do not know   Poor   Fair   Good   Excellent

2. The library should have a warm and inviting atmosphere. How would you rate the atmosphere of this library?

    Poor_____ Fair _____ Good _____ Excellent _____

3. Adequacy of the collection for the subjects at the grade level for which you teach.

    Poor_____ Fair _____ Good _____ Excellent _____

4. Adequacy of educational media and audio-visual equipment for your subject area(s).

    Poor_____ Fair _____ Good _____ Excellent _____

5. Effectiveness of the reference collection for your subject area(s).

    Poor_____ Fair _____ Good _____ Excellent _____

6. The library staff's efforts in giving you opportunities to suggest materials to be purchased.

    Poor_____ Fair _____ Good _____ Excellent _____

7. Based on your observations, rate the effectiveness of instruction by the library staff with your classes in library skills.

    Poor_____ Fair _____ Good _____ Excellent _____

8. What materials would you suggest be added to the library's collection?

Student Evaluation

1. The library should have a warm and inviting atmosphere. How would you rate the atmosphere of this library?

    Poor_____ Fair _____ Good _____ Excellent _____

2. On a scale of 1 - 10 (ten the most positive) how would you rank the helpfulness of the librarian(s)? _____.

3. Approximate number of times you came to the library last month. ____.

4. How many times you needed help finding materials. _____.

5. What materials would you suggest to be added to the library's collection?

6. If you did not come to the library as much as you wanted to, list the reason(s).

Library Evaluation Case Studies

Whenever the librarian cares enough to ask students, faculty and the administration of a school to help improve the library's collection and services, she will find she has gained a measure of professional respect. For the most part, patrons will treat the evaluative requests graciously and will respond with meaningful input. The whole process will lead to a sense of collaboration between the school and the library. Nothing but good can come of such a situation.

The authors believe that "doable" suggestions from students and staff should be printed and posted, one at a time, on a bulletin board in the library. Progress or actions leading towards the fulfillment of these requests should also be posted. A summary sheet of completed requests should be part of the display.

Case 1

Student Request:

"More stuff on us that we can read."
"Pictures to." [sic]

(We found this to mean more illustrated materials on the human body; growth patterns; changes; anatomy; physiology etc., at grades 4th–6th level.)

Action Taken:

List the materials ordered. Fourth through sixth grade teachers notified when the materials arrive.

Case 2

Student Request:

More time to spend in the library.

Action Taken:

Library opened during the lunch hour, and an hour after school. Teachers encouraged to bring classes to the library more frequently.

Case 3

Faculty Request:

Keep faculty current in subject areas we are teaching, and in personal interests.

Action Taken:

Library funding will be spent on an electronic database (DIALOG). Training sessions are provided with the service. Relatively inexpensive for schools. Purchase materials on teachers' interests with curricular tie-ins as funds allow. (These materials will be used.

Case 4

Principal Request:

As part of the 6th grade curriculum, I would like each student to be able to use library resources & locate current information on a topic that is of interest to them.

Action Taken:

Librarian will schedule the time to work with each 6th grade class to teach and demonstrate this objective. Teachers will invite the principal and librarian to view the finished projects.

Index